INDO-EUROPEAN FOLK-TALES
AND GREEK LEGEND

INDO-EUROPEAN FOLK-TALES
AND GREEK LEGEND

by

W. R. HALLIDAY

M.A., B.Litt. (Oxon.), Hon. LL.D. (Glasgow)

Principal of King's College, London

THE GRAY LECTURES 1932

CAMBRIDGE
AT THE UNIVERSITY PRESS
1933

CAMBRIDGE
UNIVERSITY PRESS

University Printing House, Cambridge CB2 8BS, United Kingdom

Cambridge University Press is part of the University of Cambridge.

It furthers the University's mission by disseminating knowledge in the pursuit of education, learning and research at the highest international levels of excellence.

www.cambridge.org
Information on this title: www.cambridge.org/9781107679085

© Cambridge University Press 1933

First published 1933
First paperback edition 2014

A catalogue record for this publication is available from the British Library

ISBN 978-1-107-67908-5 Paperback

CONTENTS

PREFACE

In their published form these lectures, which were delivered on the Gray foundation in 1932, have undergone some expansion and rearrangement. Thus the second chapter elaborates the reasons for views as to the way in which folk-tales are modified in the course of transmission from country to country and in the process of perpetuation by oral tradition, which were assumed as working hypotheses for the purpose of the spoken lectures. Parts also of Chapter III represent an addition. Chapter V appears here in the extended form in which it was read as a paper to the Hellenic Society in 1931. Chapter VII is an addition based upon a paper published some years ago in *Annals of Archaeology and Anthropology*.

Professor Nilsson's Sather Lectures on *The Mycenaean Origin of Greek Mythology* came into my hands only after these lectures had been prepared for delivery. In detail, for instance as regards the legend of Perseus, there are points about which we disagree, but in general I have been gratified to find the measure of substantial agreement between our views as to the evidential value of legend. In particular, I would emphasise that the scepticism which we share as to the evidential value of legendary genealogy and chronology was reached quite independently, nor did I know, until after my own lectures were written, that his view of "folk-memory" and its limitations would so closely coincide with mine.

W. R. HALLIDAY

King's College, London
Feb. 8, 1933

CHAPTER I

MYTH, FAIRY TALE AND LEGEND

It may be that to some the serious study of popular myths, legends and fairy tales will seem a waste of labour upon trifles of no account. To others it will perhaps appear but as an ill-starred attempt to break butterflies of fragile iridescent beauty upon the cumbrous wheel of pedantry. To these last the answer is that the urge of human curiosity is irresistible, for in proportion as things excite our pleasure and interest we are forced to find out all we can about them. But so far, the critics may be allowed to be in the right, that it is from the recognition that folk-tales are genuinely works of art, if of a simple and relatively unsophisticated kind, that our study of them should start. Whatever secondary interests may arise from our procedure of analysis, dissection and comparison—they are primarily worth attention as in themselves creations of the human imagination, often beautiful and almost always interesting. Especially is this true of Greek legend, for as creative artists the Greeks were supreme. In another chapter we shall examine the Greek tale of *Swallow and Nightingale*. The elements from which the story has sprung can be shown to be the common property of European folk-lore, and even the embroidery of the tale is derived from the stock motifs of Indo-European *märchen*. But do not let it be supposed that analysis of this kind has explained

away the work of art. Though the details can be illustrated from the folk-lore of other countries, the story
itself is the unique product of the Greek genius. The
material may be common property, but the work of art
is not.

It is mainly, however, with the secondary interest of
popular stories that we are here concerned, not with their
aesthetic appreciation, and we shall find them, like other
things terrestrial, to be subject to growth, development
and decay. For, though as works of art they are the
products of the invention of individual genius, they have
become common property, and, except where they have
been given the permanence of written record, are consequently liable to be modified by the faulty memories,
the desire for innovation, the artistic skill or lack of skill
of those upon whose lips they live. Popular stories, as
we shall see, thus undergo modification at the hands of
the folk. They have been modified, too, by the work of
scholars and others who have been interested in their
content. Particularly is this true of what is generally
called Greek mythology, for it reaches us in a literary
tradition in which the stories have been worked over
again and again, often tendenciously, from the point of
view of some theory as to their character or purport. In
this field the comparative study of popular tales may be
of special service by indicating some of the material out
of which the Greek stories were made. By enabling us
to see what parts of them fall into forms which are
characteristic of primitive popular imagination, it may
make it possible to guess in some cases what elements in

2

a story are genuinely old. Finally, a wider experience of how popular stories in general are transmitted and are modified in the process of transmission may confer a juster appreciation of their evidential value for Greek historical or religious origins. That this is no small gain can hardly be doubted, for of all kinds of evidence, legend is the most difficult to handle. Its evaluation is in itself a complicated business, and the results must always be uncertain. They are, to tell the truth, no more than guesses—guesses which, of course, are most likely to be right when they are founded upon wide knowledge and experience. For in the long run the conclusions are necessarily based upon subjective impressions which are not controllable by completely objective tests.

The Greek stories, as we have them, have been continuously worked over from very early times and, indeed, all the once fashionable attempts to give an explanation of legend as possessing some hidden esoteric meaning were anticipated in classical antiquity. As early as the fifth century B.C. Metrodorus of Lampsacus was putting forward the doctrine which inspires the earlier volumes of Roscher's *Lexikon*, that all Greek legend is disguised cosmological myth and consists essentially of highly obscure talk about the weather. The view that the gods and goddesses of Olympus were allegorical representations of natural phenomena was adopted by the Stoics, and in later antiquity, when under Oriental influences sun worship became fashionable, people like Macrobius anticipated Max Müller in discovering the Sun God beneath every divine personage.

Rationalism has almost as long a history. The idea that the miraculous element in legend is mere trimming invented by poetic fancy, and that common sense, aided in some cases by etymological speculation, can get behind it to the facts, is as old as Herodotus, who opens his history with the earliest politico-romantic clashes between Europe and Asia as illustrated by his interpretation of the stories of Io and Europa. A younger contemporary, Herodorus of Pontic Heraclea, wrote a similarly rationalised account of the adventures of Heracles and, as is shown by its frequent citation in the Scholia to Apollonius Rhodius, of the history of the voyage of the Argo. This school of interpretation reaches its fine flowering in the dry materialism of Palaephatus περὶ ἀπίστων, of which portions have survived, a work completely in the spirit of our eighteenth-century rationalism. It explains, for example, how Actaeon was really a young blood who was ruined by the expenses of maintaining his pack of hounds.

The present fashion is nearest to that of Euhemerus as represented in Diodorus, where legend is treated less as containing a certain element of historical fact than as an accurate historical record of events. This last approach, though faulty in its extreme form, is the nearest to the right way of looking at the matter. It will be generally agreed to-day that a legend must be approached on its own merits and not as a riddle which conceals some hidden meaning. Indeed, it is now pretty generally accepted that all those methods of interpretation are liable to lead astray which begin by assuming that every-

4

thing means something other than it says, and then juggle with fanciful ingenuity until all these hidden meanings miraculously turn out to signify the same thing in the end. For this release from the allegorical method, which has a long history stretching back through the Middle Ages and the Christian fathers to later classical antiquity, we have the comparative study of mythology largely to thank. It is true that, in its initial stages, it was itself given to these ingenious and thankless pursuits, but the absurdity of supposing that our nursery tales were all sun myths, that Little Red Riding Hood represented the setting sun and the wolf the black cloud with its flashing teeth of lightning, and so on, did much to give the quietus to the allegorical method. And in England the comparative method was handled by a master artist in controversy, that bonnie fighter, Andrew Lang.

To-day at any rate no apology is needed for approaching folk-tales as stories and not as allegories. For convenience they may be classified into three main categories—myths, *märchen* or fairy tales, and legends. These categories, however, though convenient are not exclusive. Legend may comprise elements derived from myth or fairy tale, and in the sense that legend, like myth, may be aetiological, legend and myth may overlap.

Myths represent the answers given by the human imagination to the problems of how things came to be. How were Earth and Sky created or how did evil enter the world? The major problems of human experience pose identical questions everywhere, and it need not surprise us in consequence that the replies in different parts of the world are very similar—that, for example, the stories of *Uranus and Gaea* or of *Pandora and the Box* should have close analogies in the Antipodes. Myth then represents the first response of the human mind to that sense of wonder, which, as Aristotle tells us, is the root of philosophy.[1] It attempts to answer by imagination the questions which science later seeks to solve by inductive reasoning. In Greece, indeed, as Professor Cornford has taught us to appreciate, the Hesiodic cosmogony was the direct antecedent of the first scientific speculations of the Ionian philosophers.

If myth represents an early and simple form of science, *märchen* or fairy story represents the similar antecedent of imaginative literature. It has no ulterior object, as a rule, except to afford entertainment, though it is true that certain specialised forms—e.g. the beast fable or the parable—may be used to illustrate or point a moral, just as novels may be written "with a purpose". In general, however, the fairy tale has no axe to grind beyond providing an imaginative escape from the drudgery of the peasant's life, the tedium of the winter evening or the slow monotony of the long road. Its forms, of course, are simple and are necessarily circumscribed by the tastes and limited experience of an unsophisticated audience. You will naturally look in vain for subtle delineation of character or analysis of motive. The

[1] διὰ γὰρ τὸ θαυμάζειν οἱ ἄνθρωποι καὶ νῦν καὶ τὸ πρῶτον ἤρξαντο φιλοσοφεῖν, Aristotle, *Met.* i, 11, 8.

dramatis personae are unindividualised and are often un-
named, the king, the queen, the princess, etc., or, where
a hero is given a name, it is of a typical rather than an
individual kind—Jack, Claus or Hans. On the other
hand you will find considerable skill in the construction
of plot and often admirable powers of direct and econo-
mical narrative. The variety of subjects treated corresponds with the tastes of the audience. There is the
fairy tale proper, about kings and queens and how the
third son of a poor widow gains the hand of a princess or
how virtuous beauty in rags wins through ill-treatment
to happiness ever after with a royal husband. Such tales
provide the peasant with an imaginative escape from the
drudgery of real life into a world of wonder and poetic
justice. In stories of this kind the miraculous and sensational play a predominant part.

Other stories are based upon the experience of life.
Tales like *The Master Thief* make the same kind of
appeal as the picaresque novel to more sophisticated
audiences. A yet more realistic form is the droll, in
which peasant humour finds its vent in tales often pithy
but usually crude and coarse in expression, as the jokes
of the unlettered are apt to be. Burlesque, again, is a
relatively simple art. There are quite a number of tales
which are, as it were, parodies or comic counterparts to
the imaginative stories of princes and princesses. For
example, the tale of the hero who secures the cap of
darkness, shoes of swiftness and sword of sharpness is, as
it were, parodied in the tale of comic cunning of the
man who outwits his enemies into buying sham magical

7

articles, the hare that runs messages, the gold-dropping donkey and the pipe or stick which brings to life. Lastly there is the humour of sheer extravagance in the *Lügenmärchen*, an accumulation of nonsensical impossibilities. This type may possibly have developed from the nonsense prelude and conclusion with which folk-tales often begin and end—"Once upon a time when pigs spoke rhyme and monkeys chewed tobacco" or "the goat laid the eggs and the hen the kids; they loaded the cock with forty gourds, the fig tree bore roses, the rose tree wild figs" or such conclusions as "I was not there, nor were you so you needn't believe it" or "you get the corn and I the chaff." Such nonsense preludes and conclusions, by the way, have this further importance: that they emphasise explicitly the fact that the audience is fully aware that the scene of such tales is in the world of make-believe. To attempt, as some folk-lorists have done, to draw deductions of social fact from the fantastic details of fairy tale is wholly to miss the character of the stories.

If myth is the prototype of science and the fairy story the prototype of imaginative literature, legend is history of a primitive kind. It differs from fairy story in being related to some actual person, place, or social or religious phenomenon. It may so far overlap with myth that its purpose may be aetiological. Its object may be to explain the origin of an institution, place-name or social custom, or why a particular religious ceremony is performed. The classification here of myth and legend is not exclusive. Are we, for example, to call myths or legends either the "just-so story" invented to account for the

8

habits and cries of swallow, nightingale and hoopoe, or
that which explains by the story of Dionysus and the
Tyrrhenian robbers the supposed human characteristics
of the dolphin?

Or take again the legend of the origin of the Myrmidons of Aegina. The island, it will be remembered, was
depopulated by pestilence: the good king Aeacus there-
upon prayed for people, and Zeus in answer to his
prayer turned ants into men. A similar kind of story is
probably at the bottom of the statement of Philo-
stephanus in his *History of Cyprus*, that the early name
of that island was Σφήκεια because its inhabitants were
called Wasps (Schol. Lycophron, 447). These stories are
not vestiges of early totemism, but myths analogous in
purpose, though not identical in form, with such stories
as that of how Deucalion and Pyrrha repopulated the
land by throwing stones over their shoulders, i.e. explanations of how after some cataclysm the present race
of men in some particular district were created. The
particular local application here determines the form of
the myth. The legends are based upon popular etymology which derives the tribal names Myrmidons and
Sphekes from the Greek words for ants and wasps. The
same general idea, the creation of warrior folk from bees,
can be found elsewhere, but the legendary application of
the story may be different. Thus, an Irish legend of
Ballyvourney near Macroom tells how an Irish chief,
when outnumbered by his enemy, prayed to St Gobnate
who turned the bees from an adjacent beehive into
warriors. After the battle the rush beehive was found to

9

have been turned into brass and to resemble a helmet. This helmet was still in the possession of a local family in the nineteenth century, and was an object of great local reverence. Water administered from it was supposed to afford a certain viaticum to Heaven.[1] Here the myth is the same kind of story as that which accounts for the Myrmidons, but the legendary application is different. It is used to explain, not the meaning of a tribal name, but the origin of an object of local reverence, an antique helmet of beehive shape which is supposedly endowed with magical properties.

Myth and legend then necessarily overlap, and there are a number of borderline cases which do not clearly fall definitely into one or the other category. For our immediate purpose it will be convenient to restrict the use of the term "myth" to stories explanatory of the greater natural or moral phenomena, i.e. cosmological myth.

Legend belongs to the somewhat elastic category of stories founded upon fact. It has its root in some actual personality, place, institution or rite which has stimulated popular imagination. In proportion as it has so stimulated the imagination, it is likely to attract to itself picturesque additions from the stock of myth or fairy tale. The process by which the personal legend grows like a snowball should not be hidden from those who live in a University town. In Oxford certainly, and I have heard it whispered that in Cambridge too, there are

[1] Crofton Croker, *Fairy Legends and Traditions of the South of Ireland*, i, p. 246.

in every generation striking personalities round whose characteristics there tends to form a whole cycle of stories, which grow ever more elaborate, fantastic and further from the foundation of fact. It is exactly the same kind of process which gives rise to heroic legends. Legend has always a basis in some historical reality. The difficulty, however, is to know in any given case where history ends and fiction begins. It may be that an entirely fictitious story will be attached to some popular name. For example, Grimm, No. 81, tells how St Peter helped a soldier to effect miraculous cures: the soldier became conceited, tried to carry out the process on his own account and necessarily failed, with serious consequences from which St Peter rescued him when he had learned his lesson. This is a fairy story which has become attached to the name of St Peter. It has no historical content at all, though on the other hand it neither proves that St Peter was a fictitious character who never lived nor that he was really a Sun God. Here the story is known to be purely fictitious, partly because the plot is that of a well-known *märchen* with a wide distribution throughout the Indo-European area (what seems to be an adaptation of it was told of Asclepius and the priests at Troezen), and partly because we know a good many facts about St Peter. But where we have no outside source of information to use as a touchstone, the discrimination of what is the historical element in any legend is often a matter of extreme difficulty. For example, it is legitimate, in view of the discoveries at Cnossus, the bull-fighting frescoes with their pictures of male and female acrobats, and the evidences of Minoan contacts with Attica, to agree with Sir Arthur Evans that the legend of Theseus and the Minotaur is founded upon an historical contact between Attica and Crete in the Bronze Age and memories of the royal bull-ring and the ruins of the great palace with its un-Hellenic complex of buildings. But before the discovery of the archaeological evidence it would have been both impossible and inadmissible to have deduced the historical palace and bull-ring from the story of the Minotaur. Without the touchstone supplied in this case by archaeological discovery it would be quite impossible to isolate as historical the elements of probable fact from the embroidery of fiction which has collected round them.

CHAPTER II

INDO-EUROPEAN FOLK-TALES AND THE PROBLEM OF THEIR DIFFUSION

If the fairy stories of the world are considered, it can hardly be questioned that Indo-European *märchen* fall into a single group. In general character they are recognisably different from the tales of the Lower Culture in other parts of the world. In respect of certain basic ideas, such, for example, as the belief in an external soul, there may be similarities, but the stories have different plots and a different atmosphere. Indeed, it is noticeable how rapidly Indo-European stories become distorted where they have been diffused outside the main area to which they belong. This may be observed, for example, in the variants which have been thrown off southwards along the line of Arabic influence in Africa, e.g. in Zanzibar or among the Ba Ronga.

The homogeneity within the Indo-European group of stories goes deeper than resemblance of a general character. There is in fact a common stock of incidents and plots. If a representative collection of folk-tales from any two countries between Iceland and India be examined, a large proportion of the tales will be found to be common to both. In 1892 Jacobs wrote, "the nucleus in every European land, which is common to all, includes from 30 to 50 per cent.", and in the light of the knowledge which has since accumulated, the proportion would now certainly have to be set much higher. How is the existence of this common stock of stories to be explained?

At the time when Andrew Lang was successfully attacking the view that all fairy tales were degenerate forms of cosmological myths, anthropological investigation under the stimulus of the great work of Tylor and Frazer was mainly interested in similarities of custom, belief and idea in different parts of the world. These it explained as the products of independent reactions of the human mind to similar stimuli. At a certain stage of human mental development, it was argued, identical conditions will produce similar results. Under the influence of these ideas, three assumptions with regard to folk-tales gained popular currency. Firstly, the resemblances of the folk-tales of different countries were thought to be satisfactorily accounted for by coincidence and independent invention. Secondly, and associated with the first assumption, it was supposed that folk-tales were not invented by individuals, but in some unexplained and incomprehensible way were made by the folk. Like Topsy, "they growed". Thirdly, it was assumed that in the areas in which they are at present found, folk-tales are of ageless antiquity, and therefore provide sound evidence for the habits of the primitive ancestors of the people who tell them. Of these three assumptions the first and second can be shown to be untrue, and the third in consequence is extremely improbable.

Now as regards the first question raised as to whether

the homogeneity of the common stock of Indo-European tales is to be accounted for by coincidence of independent invention or by diffusion, it is essential to grasp the nature of their homogeneity. The thesis of Tylor and Frazer is sound enough as regards general ideas. The wide distribution of the belief in the external soul or the life token may well be due to similar but independent reactions of the human mind at a similar state of development in different areas. The similarity between the systems of augury practised by the early Italic peoples and the natives of Borneo [1] must be due to coincidence and not to contact with each other or with a common source. The resemblance between certain cosmological myths in widely separated areas may again be rightly explained by the fact that wonder at the same natural phenomena suggested the same kind of ideas to human curiosity at similar stages of mental and scientific development. Or again, the idea that games were first invented as a diversion to enable an army to endure the hunger and tedium of a siege might well have occurred independently to the Greeks, who ascribed the invention of draughts to Palamedes, and to the Sinhalese, who tell how Rama allayed the anxiety of Mandodari, Ravana's wife, during the siege of the capital of Ceylon by the invention of the mimic warfare of chess.

The homogeneity of stories, however, goes far deeper than similarity in general idea. The school of investigation, to which reference has been made, was

[1] See Warde Fowler, *Roman Essays and Interpretations*, pp. 146 f.

in this, as in other fields, a little liable to be satisfied with apparent resemblances and to forget that essential differences are even more important. To establish the soundness of an argument from analogy the data must be critically examined in detail and in their context. In the case of stories we must satisfy ourselves that where two tales are claimed to be variants of the same story, they are in fact identical in structure and not merely similar in a general sort of way. For example, the idea and the practice of Foundation Sacrifice, i.e. the magical ensuring of the stability of a new building by burying a human being in its foundations, is very widely distributed throughout the world, and may very well have arisen independently in different areas. Connected with it is an Indian folk-tale of the building of a tank by seven brothers and the drowning of their sister in order to fill it with water.[1] This, according to Groome,[2] provides "a striking parallel" to the ballad of *The Bridge of Arta*. But actually there is nothing common to the two stories except the idea of foundation sacrifice of which the victim is a female relative. The resemblance of the tale of the bridge at Zakho in Kurdistan[3] in so far provides a closer analogy that the building in question is also a bridge and the victim a young bride. But here again the resemblance ends. On the other hand, throughout the Balkan area is found the tale of the rash vow of the

[1] Campbell, *Santal Folk-Tales*, pp. 106–110; Bompas, *Folk-lore of the Santal Parganas*, pp. 102–106.
[2] Groome, *Gypsy Folk-Tales*, pp. 12–13.
[3] Sykes, *Dar-ul-Islam*, p. 160.

master builder to sacrifice the first person coming to the bridge and the consequent building up of his wife as a foundation sacrifice. The various forms of this tale are genuinely variants of the same story because they possess not merely a general resemblance of idea but also an identity of structure. They consist, that is to say, of an identical series of incidents arranged in the same general order of interest. Within this group there are variations of detail and, indeed, two types are distinguishable which may be labelled *The Bridge of Arta* and *The Bridge of Scutari*. The nature of the differences between these, however, and the limited and continuous area in which they both are found make it evident that one must be a variant of the other. To which priority may be given as being the original version is a matter of opinion rather than certainty. My own view is that *The Bridge of Arta* is secondary and developed from *The Bridge of Scutari* type.[1]

The idea of champions endowed with marvellous and special abilities is natural enough, and might quite easily arise independently in different countries. One need not suppose any link except coincidence between Jason's companions Heracles the strong, Polydeuces the boxer, the sons of Boreas who fly like the wind, Lynceus of the keen sight, and the similar champions of King Arthur's court who are enumerated in *The Red Book of Hergest*.[2] The stories about them are similar but not identical, and

[1] I have discussed these in *Journal of the Gypsy Lore Society*, Third Series, iv, pp. 110–114.
[2] Guest, *Mabinogion*, "*Killwych and Olwen*".

neither corresponds with the plots of the two main folk-tales about the champions, (1) *How the champions rescued the princess; which is to marry her?* and (2) the story of the hero of the magic ship and his champions, who successfully perform the tasks, defeat the king's attempt to roast them alive in an iron chamber and annihilate forces sent in their pursuit. The second of these, it is true, bears a general sort of resemblance to the tale of the Argonauts, but it is a general resemblance only. The details of the two plots are different. For the purpose of discussing variants, substantial identity of detailed structure must be established.

A story, in fact, consists of a series of incidents arranged in a logical order of interest. A general similarity of idea or the possession of a particular incident in common is not sufficient to establish a relationship between tales. But our common stock of Indo-European folk-tales displays a kind of homogeneity which will pass this test: identical combinations of incidents will be found to persist through a certain minor variation of local colour imposed by national differences or accidents of transmission. Now if a story consists of a series of incidents $A + B + C + D + E$, it may not be incredible that any single element by itself should have occurred independently to different story tellers in different parts of the world, but it is surely quite incredible that the complete series arranged in that order of sequence should have been invented more than once. Thus, the idea of a skilled archer saving a child's life by astonishing marksmanship might well occur to people anywhere: there is no reason to connect the story of how Alcon the Argonaut shot the snake which was encircling his son with such dexterity that the arrow killed the snake without injury to the boy, with the story of Wilhelm Tell. Even the idea of shooting an apple off a boy's head might occur in many places independently, and, as Child remarks, "it will scarcely be maintained that Mississippi keel-boatmen shot at apples in imitation of William Tell".[1] In consequence we cannot say that the story in Persian literature of the twelfth century of a Shah who shot an apple off his favourite's head is necessarily a variant of Wilhelm Tell. But where in a defined area, the Teutonic and Scandinavian countries, we find a series of stories in which (*a*) the hero is compelled by a tyrant to shoot at an apple on his son's head, and (*b*) meditating revenge he reserves a second shaft in case of accidents, it is impossible to believe that this particular pattern can have been invented more than once. It must have been invented in one place and have spread to others by diffusion.

Of course the variants of a story are liable to deformation owing to the accidents of transmission. The original $A + B + C + D + E$ may become $A + C + D + E$ or $A + B + D + E$ or $A + D + B + C + E$ or $A + B + X + Y + C + E$. That is to say, details may be omitted or added or transposed. But where there is substantial identity of pattern, of which in particular cases common sense should be an adequate judge, we are justified in speaking of variants of the same story. When identity of

[1] Child, *Popular Ballads of England and Scotland*, iii, pp. 14 f.

this kind can be established it is very difficult to believe that the variants can have been independently invented in separate areas. Sometimes the persistence of a particular and characteristic detail may demonstrate diffusion. Thus, the idea of a dead lover returning for his bride and riding off with her to the grave door might conceivably occur independently to poets in different lands. But when it is observed that in forty-six out of fifty-eight variants recorded in a continuous chain of countries from Russia to Iceland, the horseman says, "the moon shines bright; swift ride the dead; Love, art thou not afraid?" and the maiden replies, "I am not afraid when I am with thee", it becomes impossible to suppose that this particular detail should have been independently invented in different places. The story, in fact, is almost certainly of Slavonic origin and has passed to Iceland by diffusion.[1]

The surest guide, however, is not identity of a single detail but identity of pattern. As Cosquin was the first to point out,[2] the formula for the recovery of Aladdin's ring by the cat catching a rat and forcing it to put its tail up the nose of the sleeping villain, could not possibly have occurred independently to all the peoples of the various countries from East to West of the Indo-European area in which it is found. Real identity of plot cannot in fact be otherwise explained than by supposing that the story was invented once only and in some particular place from which it subsequently spread.

[1] Child, *op. cit.* v, No. 272.
[2] Cosquin, *Contes Populaires de Lorraine*, i, p. xi.

This brings us to the second assumption that folk-tales are in some way the creation not of individuals but of the folk. The view is based partly upon sentimentality which has led to the popular exaggeration of the aesthetic merits of all kinds of peasant art and to a misapprehension as to its true character. It has derived some support from the theories of "collective mentality" put forward by the well-known school of French sociologists represented by MM. Durkheim and Lévy Bruhl. The theories of this school are disputable in their original application to the development of primitive social institutions, and they are certainly quite inapplicable to products of conscious art. It is impossible to see how collective mentality can be capable of becoming positively articulate in the invention of an intelligent design. An artistic pattern, and that is what our stories are or originally were, can only be created consciously by an individual intellect. A committee may modify a work of art or produce that very different thing, a working compromise, but no committee was ever capable of creating an original design. A plot can only in the first place have been the invention of an individual, and to say that "the folk" composed *Chevy Chase* or invented the story of *Polyphemus* is just contrary to good sense.

It is true, of course, that the conditions of transmission of popular art have an effect upon the pattern of the original, but it is quite a mistake to suppose that, except for rare accidents, "the folk" improve the design of the original artist. An unbiassed examination of any peasant art will show that the modification which actually takes place consists in the weakening or distortion of the original patterns. The design is literally rather than intelligently followed, fragments of different designs may be inharmoniously combined, detail will be misunderstood, become atrophied and disappear. The process can be very plainly seen in the peasant embroideries of the Greek islands. In the collection brought together some years ago at Burlington House, the most obvious feature was the gradual degeneration of noble Venetian designs into conventional but meaningless patterns of harmonious colour. The fate of stories is similar. Here, too, the patterns become modified, distorted and weakened; detail is misunderstood and drops out; fragments of different patterns are mistakenly introduced.

Indeed, the effect of the transmission of stories upon their form is of more practical importance to students of folk-tale than is always realised. Stories are perpetuated or transmitted in three ways, by literature, by professional story tellers and by the oral transmission of non-professionals. By literature the form of the story is fixed. When passing from one country to another it may become modified by mistakes in translation or by deliberate artifice. Shakespeare or Boccaccio may take a popular story and give it a new turn. But once set down in writing, until that writing is lost, a story has been given a permanent and unalterable form. The next most permanent form of transmission is by the medium of the professional story teller. Here the perpetuation of stories is in the hands of a craft, sometimes hereditary and in many countries highly skilled. Such modification as the tales will undergo is likely to be the result of deliberate artifice, not of accident, and it is further likely to work in one of two directions. (1) The detail may be elaborated in accordance with some particular convention which appeals to the particular taste of the hearers; I am thinking of the sort of thing represented by the language of indirect symbols employed by the skalds. (2) The attempt may be made to construct new plots. As a rule the pride of the professional is rather in the correct preservation of the old tale; both he and his hearers put a high premium upon conservatism, and the tenacity of tradition where it is in the hands of professional bards or story tellers is very strong. Particularly is this the case where the form of the tradition or story is metrical, for, as we know from the *memoria technica* of our Latin grammars, verse helps to fix the matter firmly in the memory in an undeviating form. But when the urge for original invention does break through conservatism, and that is how great literature is first born from traditional song and story, the new lay or story is made in the first instance by fresh combinations of old matter. The coloured bricks are rearranged in a new pattern. The amount of absolutely new material added will, at any rate at first, be small. It took many centuries before a Homer was evolved, a poet who could take the traditions of countless predecessors and weave them into a single and original whole. But the structure even of Homer, whose coloured bricks, some reflecting Mycenaean conditions of life centuries before the poems were written, are of very different dates, shows that it was by originality of this kind that the body of material from which he made his epic was gradually built up.

Lastly we come to oral transmission by the folk, the conservation of stories, that is to say, among people who are illiterate and are not professional story tellers. Here we should expect the form of stories to be far less permanent and much more liable to alteration and distortion. It is, after all, our ordinary experience that, if a man tells a story to a member of his club in the morning, he is liable to get it back from some other member in the evening in an almost unrecognisable form after it has passed round a number of persons. Distortion is not so rapid nor so devastating in the story telling of more primitive circles, partly because there is there a natural pride in conservatism, partly because the tellers attach a greater importance to their task and have minds less distracted by other amusing interests, and partly because they have not the intellectual alertness and originality which tempt to deliberate embellishment. But distortion there will be, and in unskilful hands a story may in time disintegrate to the point of unintelligibility. The truth of this will be evident to those who have been called upon to annotate stories taken down from illiterates as philological material and not primarily for the interest of the tales. Both among the texts collected by Professor Dawkins from the Greek-speaking peasants of Cappadocia and among those written down by the late Dr Sampson from the narration of the Welsh Gypsies I have had to deal with tales in varying stages of disintegration,

which in some cases had gone so far as to defy reconstruction of the original plot. For obvious reasons, in
collections of folk-tales published primarily for the
interest of the stories, these unintelligible *disjecta
membra* are not included.

A story we have spoken of as a pattern of coloured
bricks, and in so far as new stories are invented under
the conditions of oral transmission, they consist of a
rearrangement of known incidents rather than the invention of new matter. This is certainly the method of
popular poetical improvisation as I am familiar with it.
In Crete the art is popular, and dexterity therein an
accomplishment much admired. But, in fact, the im-
provised poetry has little originality or invention about
it. It consists in the ready stringing together of appropriate clichés of lines and half-lines, conventional
poetical tags. Essentially it resembles the sort of Latin
verse that some of us once wrote with the aid of a
Gradus. The method of the modern father when called
upon to tell a new story in the nursery, I imagine, is
usually the same, viz. to string together with what
adroitness he may, a number of incidents from different
remembered tales. My friend, Mr Thompson, has thus
recorded his experience of the methods of Eva Gray, a
noted story teller among the English Gypsies. She told
him that she "had made up a brand new tale. 'I made
it up myself from beginning to end.' What she had done
I discovered was to invent a new plot, using incidents
from *maerchen* she already knew".[1]

[1] *Journal of the Gypsy Lore Society*, Third Series, i, p. 136.

25

There is a well-known tale of *The Silent Princess*, the theme of which is the attempt of the hero to make the Princess speak by narrating stories which end with a problem. These problem stories are usually the *First Part of Prince Ahmed and Peri-Banou*, the *Carpenter and the Tailor and the Man of God*, and *How the Champions rescued the Princess*. Here you have a story frame with three self-contained sub-stories. Obviously they are separable, and each of the sub-stories may be told independently of the story frame—as indeed they often are. Equally any other story ending with a difficult problem as to which hero should justly win the heroine's hand may appropriately be substituted for any of these particular three. But a single story is similarly a pattern composed of units, which are sometimes separable. This will lead to what may be called legitimate variation. For example, as the introduction to *The Magical Flight* (Grimm, Nos. 51, 113) any incidents which will bring the hero to the home of the wizard with the marriageable daughter are appropriate. In consequence there is great variation in the form of introduction. I have noted seven different kinds in my note on a Gypsy variant;[1] a careful working through of the list of variants in Bolte and Polívka would no doubt reveal a much larger number.

Again it will strike anyone who has business with the annotation of folk-tale texts that in many cases he is dealing with groups of stories rather than with single tales. The reason for this is that some tales have parts appropriately interchangeable with others. For ex-

[1] *Journal of the Gypsy Lore Society*, Third Series, iii, p. 56.

ample, the incidents in *The Master Thief* (Grimm, No. 192) and *Little Fairly* (Grimm, No. 61) are largely interchangeable with the result that there exists a great variety of variations, all the incidents in which, however, are common to one or other of the main types. There is again the group represented by *The Robber Bridegroom*, *The Maid of the Mill* and *Fitschers Vogel* with an infinite number of sub-variations.

But under the conditions of oral transmission where the audience is not very critical nor the narrator very intelligent, part of one story will get tacked on to another mainly through the illogical process of the association of ideas. An example is provided by one of Cosquin's stories from Lorraine,[1] which is a variant of Grimm, No. 97, *The Water of Life*. In this the home of the princess and the water of life are usually to be found beyond a river, lake or sea, which must be magically crossed. This episode has brought into the French variant, through the association of ideas, the quite alien episode of the ferryman who is condemned to the perpetual task of transporting travellers across, which properly belongs to the quite different story, Grimm, No. 29. Examples of this process could easily be multiplied, and in oral transmission it is a very potent factor in the disintegration of plots.

Sometimes an incident may be dropped out completely by an unskilled narrator or survive only in some foolish trace. Thus, in a Gypsy story of *Jack the Robber*,[2] the theme of *The Master Thief* (Grimm, No. 192) is

[1] Cosquin, *Contes Populaires de Lorraine*, i, pp. 208 f.
[2] Groome, *op. cit.* pp. 48, 206.

combined with others belonging to *Little Fairly* and *The Cobbler and the Calf*. The three tests of *The Master Thief*, it will be remembered, were (1) to steal the count's horse which was guarded by a regiment of soldiers, (2) to steal the sheet when his wife and he had gone to bed, (3) to steal the parson and the sexton in a sack. Of these the third has dropped completely out of the Gypsy story. So has the second as an incident, but a trace of it survives in the incongruous and unnecessary presence of "sojers and armunition" in the bedroom of the squire and his wife.

Sometimes the teller forgets an important incident but is sufficiently intelligent to notice a gap, and attempts in consequence to patch it up. Thus, in the story of *The Six Champions* (Grimm, No. 71), it will be remembered that Archer enables Runner to waken and win the race by nicking him in the ear with an arrow or by shooting away the horse's skull upon which he has pillowed his head. In a Welsh Gypsy version the narrator forgot the incident that the Runner had so far outdistanced his competitor that he lay down to sleep. He remembered only that the issue of the race was in some way endangered and that Archer had saved the situation. Instead, therefore, of making Shoot-well shoot away Runwell's pillow in the nick of time, he is reduced to the tame and unsportsmanlike *dénouement*. "They raced, 'Wait a bit, the old witch is beating him', exclaimed Shoot-well to Frosty. Shoot-well shot a dart into her knee and Run-well beat her."[1]

[1] *Journal of the Gypsy Lore Society*, Third Series, ii, p. 51.

It has been shown that stories are invented once only and are spread by diffusion, that they must have been invented in the first place by individuals, though in the course of oral transmission they are liable to modification, and that the tendency of this modification is in the direction of distortion and disintegration. Upon the whole this process of disintegration is likely to be more rapid where society as a whole is more advanced. The more simple the stage of society, the more continuous is hereditary tradition, and the stronger is the force of conservation. In the course of diffusion, stories also undergo modification of a kind not yet discussed, a modification not of structure but of colouring. For there is inevitably a tendency for the narrators to give to them the local colour of their own national conditions and social life. For the moment it is convenient to note the fact, reserving its discussion until later.

We may now turn to the third assumption, that the details of fairy stories are sound evidence for the primitive habits and customs of the forefathers of the people who tell them. Clearly that can only be the case if we are quite sure either that the story originated among these people and did not come to them from elsewhere, or else that the detail in question belongs to the element of local colour given to the tale in this particular area alone. But even if either of these conditions be fulfilled, it will by no means follow that the deduction is sound. As we have already noticed, the fairy tale is deliberately fantastic and deals with a world of make-believe (see p. 8 above). The habit of cannibalism cannot safely be postulated of the primitive ancestors of Greeks and Albanians because these people are fond of stories of man-eating ogres.

It must further be remembered that the matter of folk-tale or folk-lore is not all of great antiquity. On the contrary it is continuously receiving additions and modifications from the ideas, learning and literature of the more sophisticated elements in society which filter down, sometimes in very distorted form, to the lower strata. Literature, as we shall presently see, exercises a very potent influence upon the oral tradition of folk-tales. It is true that it is not always possible to trace the relative age of the strata when handling folk-lore material unless we have some literary evidence by which to date it, but that does not justify the position that folk-lore is unstratified and that it is therefore legitimate to regard everything which appears in oral tradition as possessing ageless antiquity. A feature in Slavonic stories is the hut of the Baba Yaga or witch, which revolves upon a cock's foot. This definitely belongs to local colour and occurs in stories belonging to the Russian or adjacent areas. But to suggest that this remarkable structure has a real connection with the form of hut in which the Neolithic inhabitants of Russia once lived is to ascribe to "folk memory" an improbable tenacity. The Baba Yaga's hut may be just a fantastic invention, so good and appropriate that it established itself. But if it has an origin external to the story teller's imagination, it is far more probably to be found in the stories of the magical rotating palace of the Byzantine Emperor of medieval literature[1] than in social habits of the Neolithic Age.

It has been shown that stories are spread by diffusion; are we then to look for some single source from which they have spread? That the original reservoir of Indo-European stories was India and that they have passed thence to western lands was the view of the Orientalist Benfey, which was developed with whole-hearted zeal by the late Emmanuel Cosquin. The theory, however, is difficult to accept upon general grounds of common sense. It cannot be supposed that the natives of India alone of mankind originally possessed the faculty of story telling. Stories have always been told all over the world, and they have been circulated by interchange. Already we have had occasion to quote instances of plots with a limited distribution; *The Bridge of Arta*, *Wilhelm Tell*, *The Dead Lover's return for his Bride*, all these have a distribution limited to Europe. Except for a single Korean variant from the Far East, the tale of *Polyphemus*, which has been known in Europe since the days of Homer, seems not to have travelled farther east than Persia and the area of *The Arabian Nights*, and no Indian version is known to Bolte and Polívka or Hackman.[2] It provides an example of a story which seems

---

[1] See the references in Child, *op. cit.* i, pp. 274–288. Some interesting matter upon the Throne of Chosroes and medieval magical buildings will be found in Saxl, "Frühes Christentum und spätes Heidentum in ihren künstlerischen Ausdrucksformen", *Wiener Jahrbuch für Kunstgeschichte*, ii (xvi), 1923.

[2] Bolte and Polívka, *Anmerkungen zu den Kinder- und Hausmärchen der Brüder Grimm*, iii, p. 378.

definitely to have travelled eastwards from the West. Further, it must be noticed that Cosquin's methods of argument are often open to criticism. If a modern oral version of a story is recorded from India, he assumes that the Indian origin of the story is proved. A great many, however, of his Indian versions have clearly entered India with Islam. It may be true, as he contends,[1] that the occurrence of words of Arabic origin in a story does not prove the Arabic origin of that particular story, but the general use of Arabic words, such as *nasib* "fate", *ghul*, *fakir*, etc., over a considerable area must point to a strong general influence and make it probable that Northern India has many of its stories from a Moslem source. Often Cosquin displays the indiscretion as well as the zeal of a prophet. He is content sometimes to base Indian priority on the fact that the separate incidents of a story are found in different combinations in India. An example is *The Herdsman*, the particular plot of which has in fact a distribution limited to Europe, though separate incidents belonging to this plot are found in other combinations in Avar and Indian stories.[2] Or again, if he has traced a variant of a story to the Middle East, its Indian origin, he tells us, must be assumed. Not the sole example of his application of this method of argument is the story of how a man sits down by a spring and sighs "Oh"; immediately a fearsome

[1] Cosquin, *Contes Indiens et l'Occident*, p. 139.

[2] Cosquin, *Contes Populaires de Lorraine*, No. 43, ii, pp. 93–97; Bolte and Polívka, *op. cit.* iii, p. 113, n. 4; Hartland, *Legend of Perseus*, iii, pp. 3–16; *Journal of the Gypsy Lore Society*, Third Series, iv, pp. 157–158.

being appears and says, "You called me; Oh is my name". This incident does not occur in Northern and Western Europe but is very popular in the Balkans and Middle East. Cosquin claims an Indian origin for it but in fact can cite no example farther east than the Caucasus![1]

The case for an Indian origin of all Indo-European fairy tales then is *à priori* unlikely; it does not correspond with known facts, and many of the arguments advanced in particular cases are faulty. One must rather suppose that all over the area stories have originated in different centres of distribution. Some have passed eastwards and some westwards; some have extended over the whole area; the distribution of others is limited. It is true nevertheless that the greater part of the folk-tales of modern Europe have come from the East, and there has been a drift of stories from East to West. This can be traced in literature. It was mainly between the ninth and thirteenth centuries after Christ that the chief invasion of Oriental stories took place. The great collections of Indian stories were then translated into Arabic and Persian, and from the Middle East they were brought to Europe. During these centuries the larger part of the Indo-European area was dominated by two great civilisations, each of which was essentially an international society with a unity based upon a single common religion. In both, pilgrimage, the Haj and the Christian pilgrimage to Jerusalem, promoted homo-

[1] Cosquin, *Études Folkloriques*, pp. 532–542; Dawkins, *Modern Greek in Asia Minor*, p. 228; Bolte and Polívka, *op. cit.* ii, p. 63.

geneity. The actual geographical interlocking of Moslem and Christian civilisations was closer than is sometimes remembered. Spain was conquered by Islam in the eighth century and Sicily in the ninth.

Between Christendom and Islam there was close and continuous contact. The world's trade still centred on the Eastern Mediterranean. The long series of the Saracen wars of Byzantium provided for a constant infiltration of Eastern influences, particularly as prisoners, upon either side, were often released or exchanged after considerable periods of not too stringent captivity. The Pilgrimage to Jerusalem brought representatives of the whole of Western Europe into the Levant, and the Crusaders brought back with them to the West stories learned in the East. Upon both sides there grew up epics or romances of the Border Wars, the *Chanson de Roland*, *Digenes Akritas* or the Moslem epic of *Siddi Battal*. As may be seen in parts of *The Arabian Nights* the conventions of chivalry were known in the East as well as in the West, and it is even possible, as Hasluck suggested, that Western conceptions of chivalry owe something to Persian ideas.

During this period nearly all the drolls now in circulation, the tales of intrigue and of the wiles of women, and many of the romantic themes passed into European folklore. Some of the Eastern collections of tales were translated and provided the popular literature of the time; an example is *The History of the Seven Wise Masters*. The material of the Eastern story books was also largely incorporated in the collections of anecdotes for use in popular sermons, from the *Gesta Romanorum* and the *Disciplina Clericalis* down to Pauli's *Schimpf und Ernst*.

It may be asked, however, why was it that these Oriental stories so largely ousted the native variety? The answer, I think, is mainly because they were written down. They had the permanence and the form of literature and, owing to the disintegrating influences which we have noticed to be characteristic of oral transmission, they were better stories than those which they displaced. Whatever may be true of currency, good stories will drive out bad. The influence of literature upon folk-lore in general and folk-tale in particular is not always appreciated at its full value, though we have only to think of the enormous influence exercised by Perrault's *Tales of Mother Goose* or translations of *The Arabian Nights* to remind ourselves how potent it can be. Nor is it confined to the literate. A pleasant example is provided by the Gypsy version of *Ali Baba and the Forty Thieves*, in which the password is "Taĉo yek'", *Anglice*, "Safe'un". As Dr Sampson acutely noticed, the story must derive from a book in which "Sesame" was printed with the long ſ of eighteenth-century typography. The indifferent scholar who was reading it out mistook it for an "f" and "Sefame" for a dissyllable. Again, in a modern Cretan story of "the plant that gives double sight", the word used is κελπέρη, a word unknown to Greek vocabulary. In the *fabliaux*, however, in which the story is a favourite, the plant is *kerpel*, chervil. Of this κελπέρη is a metathesised form, and

3-2

clearly the Greek story is ultimately dependent on the written story.[1] Elsewhere I have examined an oral legend collected in Asia Minor in the nineteenth century and a Byzantine carol, both of which are ultimately derived from a literary forgery of the eighth or ninth century after Christ, the *Life of St Basil* by the Pseudo-Amphilochius.[2] Among the tales collected by Dr Sampson from Matthew Wood is a debased version of Marryat's novel, *Snarley-yow*,[3] and Miss Lyster has recorded a local legend at Llanrwst which is obviously derived from Watts-Dunton's novel, *Aylwin*.[4] In view of the influence of literature upon popular tales, of which these are but a few examples, it is legitimate to suppose that the reason for the predominance of Oriental types of story in European folk-lore from the medieval period onwards was the introduction of Oriental story books into Europe and the great use made of the material contained in them by European writers, e.g. the authors of *fabliaux* and *novelle*.

The history of a large number of stories can be traced in literature which can be dated. Many stories in circulation, however, are not recorded in literature; can any deductions be made as to their origin or the direction of their movement? Within certain limits it is possible to apply certain tests, though they are delicate of application under the conditions of the evidence. For one thing, we can never be sure even if we have read all the obvious

[1] Kretschmer, Λαογραφία, vii, 1923, pp. 18–24.
[2] Halliday, *Folk-lore Studies*, p. 49.
[3] *Journal of the Gypsy Lore Society*, Third Series, iii, pp. 1, 94.
[4] *Journal of the Gypsy Lore Society*, Third Series, v, p. 142.

collections of tales from a particular country, that these include all the stories told in that country. An argument based on the absence of a variant may be based only upon our ignorance. The possibility of making sound deductions, however, will be improved if annotators now devote themselves to regional study rather than aim at compiling a random series of references from all over the Indo-European area. For the broad field a reference to Bolte and Polívka with any supplement, if the author is fortunate enough to know any, will be ample. But he should give us all the variants known to him in the country of his study, and he should have a special knowledge of and give special attention to the tales of the countries in immediate cultural relationship with it, noting carefully in each case any changes in the variants. For example, the annotator of modern Greek folk-tales should have a special knowledge of the stories of Persia to which, through Turkish, the Greek tales are deeply indebted. To take but two illustrations, the "Arab" or black negro ogre of Greek stories has an upper lip which stretches to the heavens while his lower lip touches the earth. This is a Persian literary commonplace for negro ugliness. Thus Sadi speaks of a slave "who was a negro, and whose upper lip ascended above his nostrils and whose lower lip hung down upon his collar. His form was such that the demon Sakhr would have fled at his appearance".[1] Again, in Greek folk-tales the king has regularly his council of twelve (δωδεκάδα) which corresponds to no historical fact in medieval Greece.

[1] *Gulistan of Sadi*, trans. by Eastwick, chap. i, story XL, p. 71.

But in Persia, writing in 1571, D'Alessandri says, "the council is really one body in which the king is sole President, with the intervention of twelve sultans, men of long experience in affairs of state".[1]

The clue to the source of a story may lie in some peculiar detail which elsewhere has been misunderstood. A pretty example is provided by "Open Sesame". The European versions are clearly secondary to *The Arabian Nights*. In oral tradition the story tends to break down through misunderstanding. The password will become *Semsin* or some meaningless word. Or again, the narrator will remember that a plant was involved but forget the name of it, and the password will become "Open Hyacinth", "Open Rose" or "Open Tree". In some cases it degenerates into a mere "Open Mountain" or "Open Rock". The late F. W. Hasluck pointed out that "Open Sesame" could only have arisen in a country east of the Mediterranean. For "Sesame" is used as the charm for opening because sesame oil is used for oiling locks, just as in a Turkish story *madchun*, the name of a kind of stickjaw, is used as a charm to make things stick together.[2] But since on the shores of the Mediterranean sesame cannot compete with olive, it follows that the story was invented further east. Only one Indian variant from Kashmir[3] is known to me, and this contains a meaningless password, presumably a

---

[1] *A Narrative of Italian Travels in Persia in the XVth and XVIth centuries*, trans. and ed. Grey, Hakluyt Society, 1873, p. 220.

[2] Kunoz, *Turkische Volksmärchen aus Stambul*, p. 370.

[3] Knowles, *Folk-tales of Kashmir*, p. 267.

degeneration like the similar European variants. "Open Sesame" would, therefore, seem to have been invented in the Middle East beyond the olive lands and to have passed thence both into Europe and into India.

A vaguer indication of the movement of a story, and one to be used with caution, is the misunderstanding of some alien institution. For example, a story originating in a polygamous country will allow the hero to win and marry several wives. In a monogamous country such conduct is not becoming a hero, and brothers or faithful companions have to be provided to take all but one of the damsels off his hands. Where this occurs, it is fair argument that the second is the weaker form of the story and the first the original. A possible indication along these sorts of lines is evidence of Buddhist influence in emphasis upon the merit of kindness to animals. This, however, is an indication of much greater uncertainty than readers of Cosquin might suppose, for Buddhists have by no means a monopoly in feeling that kindness to animals is befitting a hero and will meet with reward.

Some weight may perhaps be placed upon the relative popularity of particular stories and incidents in particular areas, so long as it is remembered that we cannot be sure that the stories oftenest told have been oftenest recorded. Where, however, as is often the case, a story or incident is popular within an area but tends to become misunderstood and to degenerate in form the further it gets from that area, there seem to be strong grounds for locating its origin. An example is provided by the incident of the hero's meeting in the underworld a white and a black

39

ram, one of which will carry him to the upper earth. He jumps upon the wrong one and gets carried to a world yet lower than the underworld. This incident is popular in the Middle East and occurs among the Greeks of Asia Minor, the Avars of the Caucasus, the Armenians and, in an altered form, the Georgians. Along the northern route into Europe it is found in Turkish, Greek and Czech stories, on the southern among the Arabs of Aleppo and in two Moorish versions.[1] The further west it gets, the more it is liable to deformation. Similarly the tale of the *Three Orange Peris* is very popular in the Eastern Mediterranean, and from thence it obviously spread over Southern Europe. It is rare or unknown in Northern Europe. There are Indian stories which present certain similarities, but there is no Indian variant of the identical combination of incidents which make it up.

Changes, like that of a polygamous hero into a provider of brides for brothers and friends, are dictated by differences of social custom. In this case a desire for modification, sometimes a misunderstanding of alien ways, will lead to alteration. Under the conditions of oral transmission a people will always set something of their own stamp upon their tales. The simple proof is that experience will often be able to make a shrewd guess, upon reading through an undoctored version of a story, from what area, if not from what country it hails. The witch's hut which revolves upon a cock's foot will

[1] For the references see Cosquin, *Contes Indiens et l'Occident*, pp. 486–494.

brand a story at once as Russian or as belonging to the Slavonic area. The mace as a hero's weapon is very characteristic of the Magyar area. In the stories of the Welsh Gypsies "the squire" tends to take the place of the king, and in a version of *Prince Ahmed and Peri Banou* ultimately derived from *The Arabian Nights*, the *peris* of the book have become "little women and little men beautifully dressed in the old-fashioned style", i.e. are modelled upon the popular conception of British fairies. It is natural, of course, that each people should tell their stories with a colouring derived from their particular conditions of life.

Equally natural, if more subtle and elusive, is the difference in national ethos. For example, there is a larger element of rationalism in German *märchen* than in Slavonic tales. The magical animal of the Slavonic story is likely in the German variant to turn out to be really, after all, a human being who has been temporarily transformed by an enchanter into animal form.[1]

[1] These differences in ethos between Russian and German tales are well brought out in A. von Löwis, *Der Held im deutschen und russischen Märchen*, 1912.

CHAPTER III

SOME EARLY CORRESPONDENCES BETWEEN
GREEK AND INDIAN STORIES

What is generally called Greek mythology consists of a
comparatively small number of cosmological myths and
a large store of legends. That the Greeks told fairy
stories we may suppose, and we have the authority of
Plato for the fact that foolish nurses frightened their
infant charges with terrifying tales. We know of Gello,
the vampire witch who sucked infants' blood, and the
stupid Lamia, with similar unpleasant propensities, who,
like the witches of Lapland, had detachable eyes which
she kept in a box, and, like other foolish ogres and
ogresses of fairy tale, could only count up to five. No
doubt this enabled the astute hero or heroine, as in the
analogous stories, to escape after setting her a task
beyond her powers of arithmetic. The Milesian and
Sybaritic tales, to which we possess allusions, were quite
evidently modelled upon drolls, and to this same branch
of folk-tale belong a number of characters, Morichus,
Praxilla, Meletius or Margites, "noodles", to use
Clouston's label, of whom we have knowledge through
a number of proverbial sayings. The familiar types of
popular story were then probably current in the ancient
Greek world, but except for Aesop's fables we have no
Greek folk-tales as such. The only example, I believe,
in classical literature of a fairy story told as such is the

42

tale of *Cupid and Psyche*, which is narrated by the old woman in the brigand's cave in the *Metamorphoses* of Apuleius. But if we have no ancient Greek folk-tales, there are, on the other hand, embedded in Greek legend a considerable number of incidents which belong to Indo-European *märchen*. What in fact we have are not the fairy stories which the Greeks must have told, but Greek legends in which elements belonging to fairy tale have been incorporated or adapted.

The occurrence in Greek legend of isolated incidents common to Eastern and Western folk-tale might be susceptible of one of two explanations. We have seen in the last chapter that before postulating a single origin and diffusion, instead of coincidence of invention, as the cause of similarity between two tales, it is necessary to have identity of pattern of sufficient length and complexity. A single idea or incident is not a safe basis for argument. It might be argued that the story of how Daedalus, jealous of his nephew's invention of the saw, hurled him from the cliff of the Acropolis, may appear to be a variant of *The Jealous Architect and His Apprentice*,[1] but that such a story could well have been invented more than once; indeed, that it might have been independently invented wherever the peculiarities of the artistic temperament had attracted popular attention. The incident of how the night-clothes, the caps or the positions in bed of the sleeping children were changed with the result that the murderess killed her own children

[1] For this widespread legend see Crooke, *Folk-lore*, xxix, pp. 219 f.; Hasluck, *Folk-lore*, xxx, pp. 134–135.

by mistake, which occurs in the Greek story of *Aedon* and is familiar in fairy tale, might by itself have occurred to more than one inventive story teller. The idea of rejuvenation by cutting up an old man and boiling him, as Medea promised to Aeson, occurs in Grimm (No. 81), but it is in a different context. The idea might have been thought of independently more than once.

The number of such coincident inventions, however, is likely to cause the honest enquirer a little uneasiness about the probable truth of this solution, and, as we shall shortly see, there are some identities extending to patterns which it is difficult to ascribe with any plausibility to coincidence of invention. The next obvious possibility is that all these incidents and stories which are common to Greek and Eastern legend and folk-tale are of Greek invention. In Pausanias (x, 33, 9) there is a version of the *Bed Gelert* story, which occurs also in the *Jatakas*. Pausanias provides the earliest attested literary date for the story; it may therefore be argued that the story passed to India from the classical world. Here we are faced indeed with a very grave and serious difficulty. It is certainly true beyond reasonable doubt that certain collections of fables and stories have a very much older ancestry in the East than our earliest written records of them. There is support for this view from very characteristic forms and contexts which they have received in their earliest known versions. But the very great antiquity of the contents of the *Jatakas* depends upon inferential probability and not upon proof. The earliest extant manuscript belongs, I understand, to the fifth century of our era, but Sinhalese sculptures of the third century after Christ show that two hundred years earlier the same fables in substantially the same form were in Buddhistic circulation. It is the opinion of the Orientalists that it is probable that they go back to the teaching of Gautama himself, who adapted to his own use a pre-existing popular literary form much in the same way as Our Lord made use of parables. If this opinion is correct, the older stories in the *Jatakas* will date from at least the fifth century B.C.

If we assume that this view is correct and that the *Jatakas* do in fact go back to this early period, certain correspondences between Eastern and Western stories create difficulty. The great influx of Oriental stories into Western Europe took place, as we have seen, in the Middle Ages. But there were, of course, earlier contacts, and stories, like commodities, were certainly interchanged between East and West under the Roman Empire. An example of an Eastern story is *The Widow of Ephesus* in Petronius, and it would be easy to give instances of Oriental material in such writers as Aelian. Indeed, after the date of Alexander's conquests there is obviously no lack of opportunity for stories to circulate to and fro from the Far East to the Mediterranean, but before Alexander the channels are less obvious, and direct contact between Greece and India did not exist.

There are, however, a number of correspondences which do seem to go back to the time before Alexander. Let us first take the question of the beast fable. It is, of course, a somewhat specialised form of popular tale, and

45

its invention has been claimed by different scholars with almost equal fervour for Greece, for Palestine, for Africa and for India. For my own part, I can see no reason why the type of story should not independently have occurred to different races. The earliest recorded fable is the *Hawk and the Nightingale* in Hesiod (*Works and Days*, 202 f.). That the Hebrews employed it we know from the story of Abimelech and the election of the bramble to be the king of the trees. It is at least possible that Hebrews, Greeks and Africans should independently have evolved this kind of story. But with individual fables the case is different. It is very difficult to believe that any one particular fable is likely to have been invented more than once independently in different areas.

Aesop was said by the Greeks to have been a Phrygian slave who lived in Samos about the middle of the sixth century B.C., and the reference in Herodotus (ii, 134) shows that the *Life of Aesop*, though perhaps not in its fully developed form, was already in existence in the fifth century B.C. The frequent references in Aristophanes testify to the popularity of the fables in contemporary Athens. Socrates in prison contemplated but never carried out the composition of a literary Aesop, and actually, as far as we know, Demetrius of Phalerum was the first to publish a written collection of the fables towards the end of the fourth century B.C. This work has not survived, and our own Aesop rests upon the editions of Phaedrus in the first century after Christ and Babrius in the third. At first sight

46

it might seem that this late date sufficed to explain the Oriental correspondences, which might be supposed to be additions from Eastern sources after the conquests of Alexander. For some correspondences it is possible that this is the right explanation, but it cannot hold good for all. For although the Aesop of Demetrius of Phalerum is lost, the references of Archilochus, Solon, and above all Aristophanes, supply us with a good many titles of fables which were in circulation in the fifth century B.C. and earlier. Some of these, for example *The Eagle and the Dung beetle*, which is twice alluded to by Aristophanes (*Peace*, 135; *Lysistrata*, 695), occur also in the Eastern fable literature. It is also a point worth noticing that the device of a story frame, which the *Life of Aesop* seems to have provided as early as the fifth century, has always been held to be specially characteristic of Oriental story telling, though it was known, as is shown by *The Book of Aḥiḳar*, to the ancient Middle East.

In the Greek world the associations of the fable are with the eastern shores of the Aegean and their Levantine contacts. Aesop was himself reputed to be a slave from the Anatolian hinterland. He lived at Samos, the birthplace of Pythagoras, whom Herodotus thought to have learned his doctrine of the transmigration of souls from Egypt. Since the doctrine was not in fact native to Egypt, this can hardly be true as it stands, but it is possible that Pythagoras was indebted to Egyptian channels though not to Egyptian sources. The reference of Archilochus to *The Ape and the Fox*, which shows the

47

fable at home in Ionia before the reputed date of Aesop, is the earliest reference to the monkey in European literature. This fable, at least, can hardly have been invented by people to whom monkeys were quite unfamiliar. An Anatolian centre for the distribution of the fable in Greece is not inconsistent with the Hesiodic reference, for that poet's father came, as he tells us, from Aeolian Cyme to Greece.

There are therefore a good many indications that *Aesop's Fables* were an importation into European Greece: some of them have very early counterparts in the Far East. Let us consider some other examples of early correspondence. Upon the correspondence of isolated incidents not much weight can be placed; they may be only the results of accidental coincidence;[1] but it is otherwise with three stories in Herodotus. The tale of Intaphernes' wife, the moral of which, but not the form of story, is identical with that of one version of *Althaea and Meleager* (see p. 71 below), is told by Herodotus

[1] One apparent coincidence in idea I am tempted to mention as a curiosity, though it may be purely an accident. The Tale of Troy is so familiar that we do not perhaps often reflect how very bizarre and extraordinary an invention is the ruse of the Wooden Horse. In the story of the *Taking of Joppa* in Papyrus Harris 500 (Peet, "The Legend of the Capture of Joppa and the Story of the Foredoomed Prince", *Journal of Egyptian Archaeology*, xi, pp. 225 f.) soldiers are successfully introduced into the town concealed in baskets, like Ali Baba's men in the leathern oil vessels. This incident, however, may rest upon historical fact and not upon folk-tale. The idea, however, of an artificial animal filled with armed men as an instrument of ambush occurs in the *Katha Sqrit Sagara*, when Chandamahāsena captures the King of Vatsa by means of warriors concealed in an artificial elephant (Penzer-Tawney, *The Ocean of Story*, i, pp. 133–134).

48

(iii, 119) as a Persian story. Sophocles, *Antigone*, 909–912, on the same theme that husbands can be replaced but not brothers, is doubtless directly derived from Herodotus. But real parallels occur in the East, both in the *Jatakas* and in the *Ramayana*, and coincidences of phrase suggest that both these derived from a common source. The tale in India is therefore very old.[1]

Again, the story of the behaviour of Hippocleides, who danced away his bride (Herodotus, vi, 129), is identical with that of *The Dancing Peacock* in the *Jatakas*.[2] It is difficult, I think, to regard the Greek as other than the secondary version of the two. Yet a third tale is that of *Rhampsinitus and the Two Thieves* (Herodotus, ii, 121), which is given as a piece of Egyptian history. The story was already known to Greeks and had been told of Agamedes and Trophonius in the last of the cyclic epics, the *Telegonia* of Eugammon of Cyrene. The story, which appears in the *Jatakas* and in other Indian collections, is evidently old in the East: it is one of the tales which passed with Buddhism from India to Tibet and China.[3]

Now the existence of correspondences of this kind suggests that there must be some real connection at an early date between Eastern and Western stories, in fact at a date earlier than any possibility of direct contact

[1] Pischel, *Hermes*, xxviii, pp. 465 f.
[2] Warren, *Hermes*, xxix, p. 476; Macan, *Herodotus iv–vi*, ii, pp. 304 f.
[3] See Bolte and Polívka, *Anmerkungen zu den Kinder- und Hausmärchen der Brüder Grimm*, iii, pp. 403 f.

between India and Greece. A possible explanation might be that the tales filtered through the Middle East and so reached the West by indirect channels. One Herodotus learned in Persia; another, which he heard in Egypt, had been earlier told by a Greek of Cyrene. The home of Aesop's fables is Ionia, and Ionian mercenaries not only fought the battles of Egyptians but served with distinction (witness the sword of honour brought home by the brother of Alcaeus) the monarchs of Babylonia.

But another possibility seems to me even more probable, viz. that India and Greece derived much of this common matter from a common source in the Middle East. The Empire of Darius unified the ancient civilisations of the Middle East into a single entity with a common official language, Aramaic. Its boundaries touched India on the one hand and Europe on the other. That the ancient civilisations thus fused by the Persian Empire possessed a story literature that is very old we know, though unfortunately its content has been almost wholly lost: we have a few folk-tales, romances and the *Admonitions of Ptah-hotep* from ancient Egypt, the fragments of the Gilgamesh epic from Mesopotamia, and practically nothing else of the secular literature except what has happened to be included in the Old Testament. "If we omit the scanty remains of the religious writings of the Parsees, of the whole literature of the ancient East from the Indus westwards only those fragments of Israelite-Jewish literature, which have found a place in the Canon of the Old Testament, have come down to us through literary tradition." This statement of Eduard Meyer is prompted by the discovery of the Aramaic papyrus of the *Sayings of Aḥiḳar*[1] at Elephantine, which has indicated the early date of a well-known traditional book. For if an Aramaic version of Mesopotamian antecedents was being read by Jewish mercenaries in Egypt in the fifth century B.C., the romance, and the tales and proverbs which it includes, cannot be a Hellenistic compilation as was formerly supposed. The accidental character of our evidence, of which this discovery is an example, suggests how much similar material may have been lost to us. It is at least as likely that both India and Europe owe a debt to a common source in this lost story literature, as that the early correspondences of Eastern and Western tales are due to Greece borrowing from remote India, or India from Greece. Not all fables, and certainly not all the folk-tale elements in Greek legend, are of Greek invention, though many, including some of those common to the Indo-European stock of *märchen*, may well have their origin in Greek lands. For at no time or place can we believe in a transmission that is purely one-sided, except where literature is concerned. But literature is the most powerful force in fixing the form of stories and in spreading them, and this again supports the view of a common source in the ancient Middle East, where we now know that story literature actually existed in very early times.

Turning from origins to the content of Greek legend, the paramount influence here, too, of literature

[1] For the *Sayings of Aḥiḳar* see further, chap. VII.

in fixing the forms of stories may first be noticed. Of course, for later European literature and tradition, the form was mainly fixed by Ovid, that master story teller and popular author of the Middle Ages. But I am thinking not only of the forms in later and alien literature, but of those current among the Greeks themselves. Here, in determining the vulgate, the decisive factor was Attic drama. It was not the versions of *Swallow and Nightingale* or of *Oedipus and Jocasta*, which were known to Homer, that survived, but those formulated by the plays of the Attic dramatists.

We noticed that stories common to the Indo-European area yet tend to take on local colour and a certain national or racial ethos in the different countries in which they have taken root. In Greek legend, a noticeable characteristic in the use of folk-tale incident may be noted. The Hellenic temper was rational, and the purely miraculous tends to be omitted or smoothed away. For example, the tests for the marriage of the hero to the princess, so common in fairy tale, figure frequently in Greek legend. Sometimes, it is true, the magical element is retained. Jason has to yoke the fiery bulls and sow the serpent's teeth: Admetus, to win the hand of Alcestis, must first yoke a lion and a bear to his plough. But generally in Greek legend the test takes the form of a horse race or a foot race, partly because of Greek distaste for the magical and partly, no doubt, because of the special Greek interest in athletics.

In discussing the effect of oral transmission upon the pattern of stories, we noticed that one story tends to borrow from another through the association of ideas. This influence, too, has been active in the formation of Greek legend. Thus, the story of Jason and the sowing of the dragon's teeth has been borrowed by or from the story of Cadmus, even down to the detail of causing the resulting warriors to destroy each other by throwing a stone among them and so provoking them to quarrel. This last is a *märchen* incident which occurs, for example, in Grimm, No. 20, and variants. Partly accidental, but mainly perhaps deliberate, is the close relation of the Theseus legend to that of Heracles. The hero, first of Pisistratean Athens and later of the democracy, was ἄλλος οὗτος Ἡρακλῆς. No doubt there was to start with a genuine resemblance between the tales of how the two heroes rid the land of monsters, but many of the adventures of Theseus have been deliberately modelled upon those of Heracles, and some, in which may be included the whole business of Theseus and the Amazons, have been taken straight from the legend of Heracles. Once the transference was made, there were, it is true, other causes to support the story of the Amazon invasion of Greece, viz. the common practice derived from Ionia of supposing tumuli to be Amazon graves and, in the fifth century B.C., the sentimental attraction of a mythical Oriental invasion which was a prototype of the Persian War,[1] but there is no kernel of fact here at all. It is not in that sense genuine legend, but borrowed stuff from another story. It follows that to

[1] On this see *Annals of Archaeology and Anthropology*, xi, pp. 18 f.

53

attempt to deduce any historical or pre-historical fact from the story of the campaign of the Amazons against Theseus in Europe is simply a waste of time.

The relative ease with which stories may borrow from each other on the lines of the processes observed in the case of *märchen* is an important matter to bear in mind when dealing with religious legend. Let us take, for example, a late and relatively worthless compilation, the aetiological legend about the cult of Tenes at Tenedos.[1] The cult is, of course, perfectly genuine, but the story to account for it has been put together just in the way that we have seen "new" fairy stories to be made up, i.e. it is put together on conventional lines, one incident by the association of ideas suggesting another. Tenes, the son of a king on the mainland, was tempted in vain and then falsely accused by his stepmother, as was Joseph by Potiphar's wife. He and his sister Hemithea were then exposed in a floating chest in which they drifted to Tenedos. Here an incident has been borrowed, which had possibly in the first place an hieratic origin, though it is so far altered that the exposure is of brother and sister, not of mother and infant. We may further notice a similarity to the blunders or defects which arise in the oral transmission of fairy tale—there is no motivation whatever for the inclusion of Hemithea in her brother's punishment. The story of the death of Tenes takes two forms, both again demonstrably artificial. One, the earlier, is modelled

[1] This is examined in detail in *Classical Quarterly*, xxi, pp. 37–44; see also Halliday, *The Greek Questions of Plutarch*, pp. 133 f.

directly upon the killing of Cycnus by Achilles, the other is a romantic ἐρωτικὸν πάθημα of Hellenistic date.

The incident of exposure in the floating chest, which has been borrowed by the compiler of the history of Tenes, may possibly have had an hieratic origin, i.e. have been modelled in the first place upon some piece of ritual. It occurs, however, as a punishment in fairy tale (e.g. in many of the variants of Grimm, No. 54 a), and in spite of its connection with those pre-Hellenic goddesses who have survived in legends of the leap with babe into the sea, its hieratic character is by no means certain. But, and this is a point of real importance, even if it were originally hieratic, it by no means follows that wherever it occurred in legend it would refer necessarily to some ritual practice. Incidents of hieratic legend can be borrowed, and become incorporated in another story, purely for their narrative value as sensational incidents. It is therefore very unsafe to deduce a ritual fact from a legend, unless there is evidence that such a ritual definitely existed in Greece, or unless European folk-lore provides strong and real analogies in support. Nor, again, will the evidence of a number of legendary incidents supposed to have a ritual origin be necessarily cumulative. Let us take an example. It is perhaps rightly supposed that the story of the cannibal feast of Lycaon is to be associated with the tradition of human sacrifice at the Lycaean Mount in Arcadia, which persisted as late as the time of Pausanias. But even if this deduction is right, it by no means follows that all the

55

other stories, in which this incident figures, indicate the existence of similar local rites, or of a general habit of ritual cannibalism in the royal families of pre-historic Greece. A sensational incident like the cannibal feast may be borrowed just as a sensational incident to be incorporated in a story that is not hieratic at all. Thus, there is nothing hieratic in the horrid meal of Tereus, and still less can any ritual be supposed to lurk behind the legend of Harpagus in Herodotus' account of the birth of Cyrus.

In general, of course, it is true that the very greatest caution is necessary in the handling of legendary material as evidence of historical or ritual fact. Some fact there always is, but it is exceedingly difficult to know where to look for it and how to test it. Legendary evidence cannot be treated for logical purposes as of one date or of one kind. Legends are not all of immemorial antiquity, nor are they ever, except when written down, anything but fluid. They are changing all the time. They modify one another and they borrow quite freely incidents from each other. It follows that in deducing fact from them, the argument from cumulative examples is weak and needs very careful scrutiny. For example, the fact that the Scholiast on Sophocles, *Phoenissae*, 28, gives a version in which Oedipus was exposed in a chest and cast up upon the shore of Corinth, shows only that someone, either by error or deliberately with the idea of improving the story, incorporated an incident borrowed from the legend of Perseus. It has no evidential value for any purpose. In general, what may be called the oddities of Greek mythology are of this character and of negligible value except as curios.

When a legend is used as evidence for the early existence of some ritual fact or custom the character of the legend needs first to be dissected. So far as possible, what has a local reference, which alone will be relevant, must be distinguished from folk-tale elements with a wide circulation. Further, if and when the legendary part as opposed to the folk-tale part is successfully isolated, the interpretation must not be overstated. A story which is said to "point to" something has usually very little evidential value, and where the argument is compacted with this kind of pointing the structure is usually unstable. A most frequent form of self-deception may perhaps be described algebraically. A story or a fact is a composite whole consisting of parts: let us call it $a + b + c + d$. Now unless, as is seldom the case, it is impossible for a to exist divorced from b, c and d, that is to say, unless the parts are inseparable, the presence of a will not imply necessarily the existence of $b + c + d$ as well. The real position is that the presence of a makes it possible that $b + c + d$ may also have existed.

For example, the Myrmidons whom we quoted above have sometimes been adduced as evidence that totemism was once a part of the social order of the Greek world. If our explanation is right, this proposition rests upon a mistaken notion of the character of the legend. But even if that were not so, the possession of an animal name is only one, and that not the most important, feature of totemic systems. Failing other evidence therefore it is quite unjustifiable to deduce from this, or from the superstitious abstention of the Seriphians from eating lobsters, or even from a combination of the two, that totemism, an elaborate system of social organisation into groups standing in special relationship with members of the animal and vegetable kingdoms and determining a relatively intricate system of marriage custom, ever existed in the Greek world. Did we know that totemism had flourished upon Seriphus, the explanation of the local distaste for eating lobsters would probably be rightly explained as a survival from it. But it is a very different matter to deduce the existence of totemism from this local custom or from such stories as that of the Myrmidons.

CHAPTER IV

GREEK LEGEND

We have agreed that Greek legend consists of stories told
about great men of the past, about social or political
events or institutions, or in explanation of the origin or
character of religious ritual. It is, that is to say, founded
upon a fact of some kind, though round that fact has
collected an accretion of fictitious matter.

Let us first ask ourselves what, in general, is the
tendency of tradition as a recorder of personalities or
events. So far as my knowledge of the anthropological
evidence goes, popular memory is neither very accurate
nor very tenacious, unless there exists some official
institution or class of persons whose professional duty it
is to preserve and perpetuate tribal traditions. I do not
think that you will find any people among those without
documentary records, or without some professional class
of recorders, bards or priests, whose memory of their
history goes any considerable distance back. Quite
recent events tend to be forgotten and, if dimly remembered, to get into the wrong order. In fact,
distortion and a lack of the idea of sequence are very
characteristic of popular tradition, which is likely to get
names right but is otherwise not very retentive except of
the picturesque. Aristocratic tradition in societies which
have reached that stage of culture in which heroic kings
or noble families direct the public weal is of course very

much more tenacious. Where ancestral pride flourishes, there is a strong motive for keeping alive the memory of the great deeds of forbears, and each generation, as in Republican Rome, is brought up in the ambition to be worthy of its heritage of ancestry. Most likely to be genealogically accurate and, allowing for the exaggeration of loyalty to a patron, substantially true are the traditions preserved by professional minstrels attached to the houses of chieftains. Here art, and often an hereditary craftsmanship passing from father to son, will help to stereotype and preserve the original facts. It is, perhaps, probable that in the Heroic Age the remote predecessors of Homer were minstrels of this kind, and some of the tradition which has come from them is substantially accurate. But it is impossible, except upon *à priori* grounds, to know what is theirs. Long before Homer, the centripetal forces which welded the Greek princedoms into the Greek race had begun to be operative, and after Homer the genealogies were worked over and over again in order to unify the ancestral traditions of the component parts of the Hellenic race into a single system. Even in our oldest records very little weight can safely be attached to traditional dates or to the sequence of events. In Homer himself it would be easy to show how little conscious are the poet and his audience of anachronism. This is the true explanation of many of those discrepancies in armament, ways of fighting and social institutions which have furnished the Separatists with their main arguments.

But whatever the shortcomings of popular tradition

as an accurate chronological record of historical fact, we may assume with some certainty that a person about whom a legend was told was not a fictitious character but a real person who once existed. That was the Greek view of heroic legend, and for the Greeks a "hero" was definitely a man who had lived and had become after death an object of worship. "Hero" worship is, indeed, exactly equivalent to the worship of saints. To start from the supposition that "heroes" were originally something else and not men at all, whether faded gods or functional deities or totems, is simply gratuitous. Unless there is strong reason to the contrary, it is safer to assume that the subject of a legend was a real person. There are, of course, exceptional cases and some few fictitious heroes, just as there are some fictitious Christian saints. The exceptions are mainly of two kinds. Firstly, they are persons whose legends have no content at all apart from some ritual context, and whose names have a functional significance or ritual association. I am thinking of such heroes as Eunostos, Good harvest, Echetlos, Plough-handle, Hyacinthus or Linus. A second less important class may be suspected of being legendary Mrs Harrises. Persons with colourless racial or official names—Creon the king, or, I suspect, Danaus the Danaan. Usually these are introduced to supply a necessary character in the story, like the anonymous king, prince and princess of fairy tales, or to provide a genealogical generation which for one reason or another is needed. Here might perhaps be mentioned the doublets who owe their existence to a like cause,

e.g. Pandion II of Athens, whose existence seems to be
due to the necessity of equating the chronology of Attic
with non-Attic legend.

But, speaking generally, we may presume that a hero
of legend is in nine cases out of ten a genuine person who
once lived and bore the name ascribed to him, or something like it. The qualification is necessary, because it is
not at all impossible that in some cases the names of
heroes and gods, as we have them, represent the Greek
versions of pre-Hellenic or foreign names. This, I
think, is certainly true of some divine names, Hephaestus,
Artemis, Aphrodite, etc. And here we may notice the
futility of basing far-reaching conclusions upon the
supposed meaning of the Greek forms of such names.
That is what the Greeks themselves did. For example,
they Graecised a name which sounded something like
Aphrodite and then invented a story to explain the
Greek form on the lines of popular etymology. Hence
such etymological speculations as those put forward to
explain the name Dionysus, whether ancient or modern,
are in fact so much wasted breath. Still more foolish is it
in the case of heroic persons to interpret the meaning of
their names in any esoteric sense. Penelope was not a
wild duck goddess nor a wild duck totem: the name
Coronis no doubt explains how the Just-so story about
why the Crow is black came to be attached to the history
of her relations with Apollo, and possibly accounts for
the place-name Lacereia, but she herself is a princess
of the Lapith royal house in which Coronis and Coroneus
are not uncommon names. Two of the interlocutors in

Varro's treatise on farming have been given the names Scrofa, "Sow", and Stolo, "Sucker", but these are perfectly good Roman names: Lord Hailsham is not a swine deity nor a totem in virtue of his family name.

Let us consider, for a moment, the legend of the Argonauts. That Jason was a healing god or other than a human hero seems quite a gratuitous and foolish assumption. It is natural to suppose that there was a prince called Jason, who in consequence of dynastic rivalry did actually sail from Iolcus eastward on a voyage of discovery into the Black Sea and returned thence with a foreign princess. Popular imagination has, of course, decked out this adventure with picturesque plumes borrowed from fairy tale. The Argonauts are a collection of champions who individually possess complementary magical gifts, like the champions of King Arthur's Court in *The Red Book of Hergest*, or those in the well-known fairy story (Grimm, No. 71) to which reference has been made above. The magical tests which are set for Jason's performance follow the model of fairy tale. There are those who think, though it is not altogether a convincing view, that the story of the Flight from Colchis is a rationalised version of Grimm, No. 113, *The Magical Flight*. The adventures en route mainly belong to fairy land. It is true that here there are modern Palaephati who can explain many of the miraculous episodes by common-sense rationalism. The blue clashing rocks were icebergs, and the quest of the Golden Fleece has to do with a method of extracting the precious dust from riverine gold deposits by means of fleeces.

63

Though there is no means of definite proof that these explanations are wrong, it does not seem probable that they are likely to be right. *Credat Judaeus Apella.* Roughly, most of the detail is either fairy story or in its elaboration tendencious history. Thus the lists of those who took part in the voyage were worked over again and again; for this, like the Calydonian Boar hunt, was one of the great instruments for securing a formal unification of the legends of different parts of Greece. It was also a matter of local pride that the appropriate local heroes should have taken part in these two great adventures. Similarly, though some elements may be old and correct, the geography cannot be accepted without very careful scrutiny, since it has been mainly used to indicate the antiquity of the foundations of a much later period of colonisation. In fact, there is not a great deal of history left when the trimmings are shorn off, but on the other hand, what there is, is important. Jason's voyage to the Black Sea was a real event, which helped to make history.

Here we have been dealing with a legend which, at any rate in its essentials, we know to have been current before Homer. It is an added difficulty in the evaluation of legend that we cannot always be certain that we are handling a genuine tradition of real antiquity. It follows that to piece together odd bits out of a variety of stories, without considering the character and probable historicity of each of them in its local context, is an extremely dangerous proceeding.

We have already emphasised the unsoundness of the

assumption that because folk-lore is dateless it is therefore unstratified, or in other words that all legend is of
more or less equal antiquity, and that all of it is very old.
Actually, a great deal of the material of folk-lore is quite
recent and legend is by no means uniformly antique.
Let me give a modern example. At the top of Porlock
Hill in Somerset are two large isolated' blocks of stone,
to which a legend now attaches of their having been
thrown from Hurlstone Point at the far end of Porlock
Bay. Now this story cannot be older than the Ordnance
Survey, for it was then that the Surveyor, who was not
sufficiently versed in our local dialect to recognise
Redstone in Hurtstone, invented through misapprehension the name Hurlstone. From this name, which
owes its origin to this recent mistake, the legend is
derived. Greek legends, similarly, are not all of a piece
and they may belong to very different epochs. Nor are
individual legends insusceptible of change: even in
popular tradition bits may accidentally be dropped out
and bits may be added, and in literature not seldom a new
turn is given to a tale by deliberate artifice.

Before attempting to interpret a legend, therefore,
some account must be taken of whence our knowledge of
it comes. Of course, a version preserved by Homer or
Hesiod may be assumed to have a very respectable
antiquity, and in general the antiquity of the author in
which the story occurs is a factor to which full value
must always be given. But just as in other realms of
classical scholarship, while it is profoundly untrue that
anything written in the Greek language has equal

evidential value, a Byzantine lexicographer may contain something which he obtained from a good source no longer available to us; similarly, a late and bad author may preserve a very early version of a legend. A notorious example is the imbecile Hyginus, who appears to have been an indifferent Greek scholar as well as a writer of execrable Latin. But he clearly had access to good sources and, when we can be sure of understanding what he really means, he often gives us information that we get from no other source.

That does not mean, of course, that we are to prefer the curious quiddities of late and imbecile authors or pedantic scholiasts. In practice, the sound rule is to prefer as older the version of the earlier author unless there is some definite reason, other than our desire for it to be so, to suppose that the later author's version is genuine. I should not wish to condone the type of argument which bolsters up a theory by an excerpt from some late author, merely because it happens to fit in with the writer's hypothesis and gives it a fictitious appearance of evidential value by appeal to "tradition otherwise lost". The true meaning of such a phrase as "Solinus summarising traditions otherwise lost" is rather "there is no authority except a late and inferior one for the following statement, which upon other grounds the author would like to be true".

Another class of legend must be treated with the greatest caution, and all arguments based upon combinations of its constituent parts should be regarded with the greatest suspicion, viz. legend for the formation of which there is an obvious ulterior motive. To this class belong all foundation legends. No doubt a great many may contain some elements of real fact, but all have been worked over for tendencious purposes until there is little means of discerning what is fact and what deliberate fiction. A good example is provided by the legendary history of Rhodes. A great deal of play is often made with it, both for purposes of secular and of religious history, but in fact, except that we can say that in the form in which we now have it, it is an artificial and tendencious compilation,[1] there is nothing to be done with it. It is quite hopeless, except as a pastime, to attempt to trace from it the wanderings of an alleged Thessalian cult of Zeus Triops, or to gain from it light upon the relations between Crete and Anatolia in the late Bronze and early Iron Ages. Any genuinely old material which it may contain has been so manipulated that it is now indistinguishable.

Of course, what we are calling legend, to the Greeks was the early history of their country, and in political disputes great attention was paid to historical argument. For example, in the celebrated dispute between Samos, Priene and Miletus over the ownership of Carium and Dryussa, of the fluctuations of which we have record over four and a half centuries, the Samians based their case upon alleged historical writings which were eventually pronounced to lack evidential authority.[2] Such being the use of legend, it is not surprising that it was freely

[1] See Blinkenberg in *Hermes*, xlviii, pp. 236 f. and l, pp. 272 f.
[2] See Tod, *International Arbitration*, pp. 135 f.

invented to further political claims. Of this type of propaganda the Athenians in particular were masters. The forgery in the Homeric Catalogue to support their claim to Salamis is notorious. We are told that in his successful *Oratio Deliaca* before the Amphictyons, Hyperides, "desirous of proving that the Delian Sanctuaries belonged of old time to the Athenians, has made great use of mythology".[1] When Aeschines was putting forward the Athenian claim to Amphipolis, he reminded Philip that the Athenian Acamas, when returning from the sack of Troy, had married a Thracian princess, part of whose dowry had been the district round The Nine Ways.[2] Similar, I think, is the origin of the alleged connection through Cephalus of the Attic family to which Andocides belonged with the royal house of Ithaca, and it was probably on account of this connection that Andocides, the grandfather of the orator, was sent with the Athenian fleet to the Ionian islands in 433–432 B.C.[3] Such examples might be multiplied almost indefinitely, and similar uses of legend might be illustrated from the pages of Herodotus, e.g. iv, 179, where the alleged voyage of Jason and the Argonauts to Africa is used to justify the Hellenic occupation.

We have so far been considering legends which purport to refer to secular history; another important kind of legend is religious legend. Q. Mucius Scaevola,

---

[1] Maximus Planudes, *Oratores Attici*, ii, p. 392, Didot.
[2] Aeschines, *de fals. leg.* 31.
[3] See Halliday, *The Greek Questions of Plutarch*, p. 81.

perhaps the most learned of those who held the office of
Pontifex Maximus, enunciated the orthodox Stoic view
of religion that it consisted essentially of three elements:
(1) philosophy, (2) stories which served to inspire the
fancy of poets, (3) an instrument by which the statesman
might control the ignorant populace who believed in the
literal truth of these fables. To the modern student of
religion these stories are still of greater interest and importance than is sometimes allowed. In reaction from
the view prevailing in the early nineteenth century,
when the religion of the Greeks and Romans was
evaluated simply in terms of Lemprière's dictionary, and
in consequence of the very right insistence upon the
primary importance of ritual, τὰ δρώμενα as opposed to
τὰ λεγόμενα, perhaps too little importance has lately been
assigned to the stories about divine things. A part of
them consists of myth, accounts for origins of civilisation or seeks to explain moral rather than concrete fact.
The importance of these latter stories to a student of
religion is obvious. They help us to appreciate the kind of
mental picture that the Greeks formed of their gods,
and, further, they helped the Greeks to form the mental
picture itself: for myth is not merely passive, and the
stories tend to mould the conceptions of divine personality. A part, again, of religious mythology is
legend, in the sense of being founded upon political
tendencies. The tales of the multiple amours of Zeus
and other gods, to which so many Greek thinkers
objected as unedifying, arose from the craving of various
elements in the Hellenic race for a divine ancestry, and

69

also from the centripetal tendency to bring the various stocks to the unity of a common divine origin.

But the most important kind of religious legend in the strict sense is the aetiological story arising from the concrete fact of some ritual observance. Here the value of the story will again vary to some extent in accordance with its antiquity. The explanation itself will *ex hypothesi* be unveracious, for the legend has been invented to account for some piece of antique ritual or ordinance the meaning of which is no longer understood. But if it can be dated, it will tell us what the Greeks of a particular period liked to believe about the origin of a religious observance, and sometimes it will indicate by analogy what the ritual actually was. There is also this importance about ritual legends which are really old, that just as stories about gods helped to modify their character in the minds of their worshippers, just as the embodiment of divinities in plastic form had an important influence upon moulding the popular conception of them, so the stories told to explain ritual often modified the ritual. For myth and ritual interact, and if ritual gives rise to myth, myth in turn can give rise to ritual.[1]

Folk-lore and folk-tale, as we have seen, are not static, but, like other products of human imagination, are subject to mutability, change and development. We find different versions of a story which can sometimes be arranged in relation to each other and thus show us the history of the story and its modification. Sometimes the relation of the different versions cannot be determined.

[1] See H. J. Rose, *Modern Methods in Classical Mythology.*

Let me take an example. In *Iliad*, ix, 523 f., Phoenix
tells the story of Meleager. In this version Oeneus
forgot to make offering to Artemis at the harvest-home.
The insulted goddess then stirred up strife between the
Aetolians and Curetes over the head and skin of the
Calydonian boar, and in the fighting Meleager killed
his maternal uncle. His mother, in consequence, beat on
the ground to awake the underworld powers and devoted
her son to death. Meleager, like Achilles, retired from
the fighting, but in the end, as the Curetes were on the
point of sacking the town, yielded to the entreaties of his
wife, donned his armour, sallied out and saved the city.

This is obviously an old and primitive story, though
one must suspect Phoenix of twisting the *dénouement* in
order to suit his immediate moral; for it is clear that in
the original the curse of Althaea must have had fatal
consequences. But for the rest, the incident of the
neglected fairy is a commonplace of fairy tale, e.g. in
The Sleeping Beauty (Grimm, No. 50).[1] The greater
affection for the brother than for the child or husband is
again a very old *märchen* motif both in East and West,
which perhaps has its origin in a primitive form of social
organisation in which descent is traced through the
mother, and the maternal uncle is in the special kind of
relation to nephews which in patrilinear societies is

[1] Other Greek examples are Pelias and Hera (Ap. Rhod. i, 13;
iii, 65), Tyndareus and Aphrodite (Stesich. Schol. Eur. *Or.* 249),
Naiades and Achelous (Ovid, *Met.* viii, 573–589), and late versions
of Centaurs and Lapiths (Peirithous and Ares, Bode, *Mythog.* i,
162), marriage of Peleus (Discord neglected, Bode, *Mythog.* i,
208), Lemnian deeds (Aphrodite, Bode, *Mythog.* i, 155).

held by the father to sons. The invocation of the underworld powers by beating on the ground is also a very
ancient piece of ritual. But the alternative version,
which was perhaps first given literary form in a play of
Phrynichus,[1] has an appearance of equally genuine
antiquity. In this the three Fates entered the room after
Meleager's birth. The first two blessed the babe, the
third, Atropos, laid a brand in the fire with the prophecy
that when the brand was burned up Meleager would die.
Althaea extinguished the brand and kept it. When
Meleager killed her brother she took it out, thrust it in
the fire, and Meleager immediately expired.

This version has equally primitive features; the visit
of the three Fates and their behaviour will be familiar to
any reader of fairy tale, and the belief in the life token or
external soul is primitive and of frequent occurrence in
märchen. In spite of the fact that one is given by Homer
and the other is preserved only by late authors, there is
no reason to say that either version is the older or the
original story. We have, in fact, two different versions,
both of which are declared by their subject-matter to be
very old.

Sometimes, however, the versions of a story can be
put in their order and the growth and modification of
the tale be traced. An example is provided by the tale
told to explain the habits and cries of a series of spring
migrants, nightingale, swallow, and hoopoe, which is
discussed in the following chapter. The definitive form

[1] Pausanias, x, 31, 4; Antoninus Liberalis, 2; Ovid, *Met.*
viii, 451.

of this story will be shown to have been finally fixed by a play of Sophocles, a good illustration of the influence of Attic drama in fixing the canon of established versions of Greek legend. That the Attic stage should have exercised this predominating influence is not surprising. An analogy, perhaps, is furnished by Shakespeare, whose plots are borrowed goods, though the familiar forms of these stories, since the production of his plays, are those in which he has clothed them. The popular idea of the history of Hamlet or the tale of Shylock is cast in the mould formulated by Shakespeare's adaptation. Without research no ordinary person knows what forms the stories took in the sources from which Shakespeare borrowed them. The same kind of thing happened in the case of Attic drama, and although we have sometimes record of earlier versions or know of later elaborations, it is mainly the mintage of the Athenian dramatists which was current in antiquity.

The Attic dramatists, like Shakespeare, borrowed their plots: from whence did they get them? Aeschylus carved slices from the banquets of Homer, i.e. from epic, not only from the *Iliad* and the *Odyssey*, but also from the lost epics which dealt with central themes other than the siege of Troy and the Return. What lies behind Homer is necessarily a matter of conjecture, and demonstrable certainty is unattainable, but some indications may be gleaned from the Homeric poems themselves, and the analogy provided by the history of the epic poems of other peoples may fairly establish some reasonable probabilities as to the development of epic poetry in Greece.

73

That Homer himself represents the flowering of a long literary development is shown by that finished poetic instrument, the Homeric hexameter. It is shown no less by the nature of his subject-matter. He is writing some three hundred years after the fall of Troy and some five centuries after the date at which the hegemony passed from Cnossus to Mycenae. Moreover, since it is an inevitable tendency when one gets back to the vast periods before written history to talk glibly with centuries as units, let us remind ourselves that a poet writing to-day about the Great Rebellion would be as near in time to his theme as Homer. His case would be different only because he would have continuous literary records upon which to draw, whereas Homer had nothing but the tradition preserved by epic technique.

In Homer's poems there are passages reflecting the social life and conditions of varying centuries, from those of the Orientalising period, when the poems were composed, back to the Mycenaean, and, as Professor Nilsson has pointed out, to the very earliest Mycenaean period. This, if the traditional theme goes back to Mycenaean times, is what we might expect, for the epic technique is not so unlike the technique of popular story telling which we have already discussed. Essentially, though it is upon a more skilful plane, it is the rearrangement of the pattern of coloured bricks. In the course of centuries, the poets add new incidents and new passages reflecting the conditions of their own day, while a certain number of the well-admired clichés continue to hold their own, even if in detail they have

74

become anachronisms. The survival in the Homeric poems of Mycenaean memories and clichés could only be explained on the basis of a long continuous poetic tradition.

There were other epic poets before Homer, and there were other epic poets in his day, but that is not to deny the unity of Homer nor to fail to realise that he revolutionised epic poetry by lifting it on to a different plane of literary art. Bards, of course, are mentioned in the poems, and in the society depicted by Homer the professional poet, like Demodocus, is an honoured craftsman. There are allusions to other epics with which Homer's audience were plainly familiar. The story of Meleager is introduced by Phoenix as "a tale I have in mind of old time and not of yesterday". The story of the Argo was plainly known to Homer's hearers. The tale of Bellerophon is not told at length but sketched allusively: Homer's audience will be familiar with it.

To what period do the beginnings of the development of these epic traditions go back? It is pretty certain that the Minoan kings of Cnossus spoke some language other than Greek, but we have no definite evidence whether Greek was or was not spoken by the kings of Mycenae, whether by those of the Shaft Graves or those of the great Beehive Tombs. On the other hand, the differences between the culture of the mainland and that of Crete, which are increasingly attracting attention, are moving the general opinion of scholars towards the view that Greek was the language of the mainland earlier

75

than was formerly supposed, and that at least the period known as Late Minoan III was an "Achaean" Age. Professor Nilsson has now shown the probability that most of the great themes of Greek legend go back to Mycenaean times. For his arguments in detail reference must be made to his books, but three very important considerations may be noticed which he has certainly established. Firstly, all the places with which the great legendary cycles are connected in story have been revealed by the spade to have been centres of Mycenaean civilisation. Secondly, places where archaeology shows Mycenaean culture to have been powerful and important are rich in legend, but where Mycenaean remains are scanty there is a corresponding poverty in legendary association. Thirdly, the social organisation￫ of the Homeric gods reflects, and can only reflect, Mycenaean monarchy.

If one attempts to imagine the probable course of development, it seems to me to be likely that the main cycles of Greek legend were formed in the Mycenaean period and were given shape by professional minstrels at the courts of the Mycenaean kings. The alternative hypothesis, that they were in the first instance foreign poems and legends which were translated later into Greek, would appear in the highest degree improbable, in view of all that is known of this kind of unwritten but professional song-making. This improbability is indeed a very strong argument for the view that the Mycenaeans must have spoken Greek. Why the epic tradition tended to centre round certain particular themes, above all the Siege of Troy, we cannot say. Analogy suggests that there is an element of arbitrary accident. Why Troy? There is more reason than for Roncesvaux.

After the break-up of the Mycenaean kingdoms, the epic songs became popular property. The common people, too, liked to hear the tales composed originally for the court, or perhaps one should say not the common people but the lesser chieftains. Along with the preservation of the big themes went probably a development of local legend. In the sub-Mycenaean and Geometric periods, centrifugal forces were dominant. As archaeology bears witness, separatism reigned; each area began to develop its own way of making things and ornamenting them. The Hesiodic rather than the Homeric *basileis* kept their little courts at which their minstrels perpetuated the legends of the particular tribe, area and royal family. Every tribe and area had its own store of legend and saga. As Hesiod says of the local river deities of Greece, "the names of all it were hard for a mortal man to tell, but in each case they know them who dwell round about".[1] But the history of Greece is of the warfare of centripetal and centrifugal forces. The wandering bard[2] must have done much to unify local traditions and legends, and eventually there emerged Homer and Hesiod to fix a Pan-Hellenic canon. This is the element

---

[1] Hesiod, *Theog.* 369.
[2] Here it may be noticed that legends are carried by the wandering bard and not by tribes. Apart from the silliness of its application, the theory of *Sagenverschiebung* displays an entire ignorance of how legends in fact do migrate.

of truth in Herodotus' famous dictum: "Homer and Hesiod by composing theogony for the Greeks both gave their names to the gods, discriminated their honours and their crafts and indicated their forms" (Herodotus, ii, 53).

Homer and his successors and the Hesiodic poems mainly formed the original canon of Greek mythology and legend. From the historical point of view, they represent the unification of historical traditions of the tribes which made up the Greeks into a systematised history of the Greek race. Homer, Theban epic, the cyclic poems, such works as the Hesiodic *Eoae* and *Melampodia*, these are the banquets from which the Athenian dramatists carved slices.

The work of the Hesiodic poets was in part a systematising of legend through genealogies, and just as the first Ionian philosophers carried on in a more scientific form the speculations of Hesiodic cosmogony, so the early historians or logographers carried further the work of the author of the *Eoae*. Hecataeus, Acusilaus, Pherecydes, Hellanicus and the rest endeavoured to reconstruct the early history of the Greek race and to work it into a single unity by the systematic study of genealogies. The plan of their works is normally genealogical, taking each great branch of the Greeks in turn. It was their task, as it had to some extent been the task of Hesiod before them, to make sense of scattered and sometimes discrepant traditions. For us it is often impossible to know where the work of harmonisation begins and ends, particularly in respect of chronological generations.

Then in literature came Attic drama, whose wide-spread vogue and popularity gave universal currency to the forms of story which it adopted. Between Epic and Attic drama there are, of course, the poems of Pindar, full of legendary material. But with some familiar and brilliant exceptions Pindar does not tell the stories, he alludes to them. Necessarily, therefore, he did not much influence the form of the stories themselves, though to the obscurity of many of his allusions and the necessity of commentary we owe no little of our information as to the plots of Greek legends and our knowledge of the contents of the works of the genealogists.

So far the modification of legend, whether through creative literary art or historical study, had mainly been centripetal in character, working in the direction of a Pan-Hellenic canon. In the fourth century, to some extent a centrifugal reaction took place. Already in Euripides it is possible to trace a strong local anti-quarian interest. Euripides, indeed, was a good and interested religious antiquary; an aspect of his character which might repay a little investigation, particularly as it may have a bearing on the vexed question of his religious views. In any case, from the fourth century onwards you have the development of local histories, of which the Atthidographers are examples, and inevitably an interest in local and peculiar legends. You have, too, the more sophisticated development and publication of temple records, to the greater glorification of the parti-cular religious centre and the edification of its pilgrims. I am thinking of such things as the Lindian Chronicle

79

or the Epidaurian lists of miraculous cures. In completion of, and upon the basis of these, there arose the specialist writers of treatises upon religious ritual like Socrates of Argos, or upon holy places like the two tracts of Anaxandridas about Delphi, or works like that for which Demoteles, the son of Aeschylus the Andrian, received a gold crown and a laudatory inscription from the Delians (c. 290–280). The reward was in respect of his poems dealing with the shrine and the city of the Delians, and his record of the local legends, τοὺς μύθους τοὺς ἐπιχωρίους.[1]

By the learning of Alexandrian scholars all these scattered sources were collected into compendia, mainly of two kinds. The first consists of systematic mythographies arranged usually, like the work of the older logographers, in genealogical sequence, i.e. each great branch (the Deucalionids, the Asopids, the Heraclids, etc.) being taken in turn. The main object of these encyclopaedias was to provide the necessary background of knowledge to enable schoolboys or students to master, and ordinary cultivated people to enjoy, the allusions and references to mythology in classical drama and poetry. The best example of a considerable work, which though itself of later date is based upon one of these compendia, is the *Bibliotheca* which bears the name of Apollodorus.

The second type is more miscellaneous and less encyclopaedic. It consists of collections of materials for exploitation by poetic fancy. The grouping is not by genealogies, but by subject lists of *Metamorphoses*, or

[1] Ditt. *Syll.*3 382.

80

Katasterisms, or like the work of Parthenius, which is perhaps the best surviving specimen of the genre, ἐρωτικὰ παθήματα, romantic love stories. For such works the local histories were searched, and some of them indeed were avowedly arranged as a collection of local legends, such as the lost τὰ κατὰ πόλιν μυθικά of Neanthes of Cyzicus. The contents of such compendia were, of course, more miscellaneous and disjointed than those of the first kind, and the items were selected primarily for their picturesque, sensational or romantic value as literary material.

Upon these two kinds of Alexandrian handbook a great part of the knowledge which we possess is based. Together with the uses made of them by Alexandrian poets, they provided the material for Roman poetry, and from them is also mainly derived the information given by the long line of commentators and scholiasts upon classical literature.

Exceedingly valuable for the student of Greek legend is the material which can be traced back to the great mythographical encyclopaedias of the first kind. It is thanks mainly to them that we know as much as we do of the contents of the early genealogists; of this an illustration, which can readily be checked, is the debt to Pherecydes of the work which passes under the name of Apollodorus. Of far less value was the material in the compendia of the second kind, and its almost total loss need not greatly concern us. The local legends, so far as one may judge, did not amount to much of importance or even to much that was very old. A feature which struck me when working at the *Greek Questions* of Plutarch, into which a certain amount of this kind of material has drifted, tends to confirm from another angle the view of the dominant influence of literature upon tradition. For a very strong tendency is shown for local legend in explanation of place-names, etc., to link up the locality with Homeric tradition.

Another reason why this kind of compendium is less valuable than the genealogical dictionary is that the object of the compilers was literary, not historical. Both the selection of curiosities and the form of their presentation are in harmony with the taste of the time. There is a tendency not to record legend, but to distort it in writing it up in such a way as to emphasise picturesque or romantic features, and the influence of the novel is plainly to be discerned. Indeed, wherever the romantic love element or intrigue is markedly prominent, it is legitimate to suspect a Hellenistic invention or distortion. The tale of Scylla and the purple lock of Nisus is as old as Aeschylus, but the romantic story of how her treachery was inspired by love of the invader and the punishment with which it was rewarded, a type of tale repeated of Tarpeia and in a number of subsequent local legends, I strongly suspect of being a Hellenistic addition.

There is a further source of information which has not yet been mentioned, that supplied by pictorial illustration, mainly by the designs upon Greek pottery. The evidence from this source, however, is much less reliable than is often supposed, and the structures built upon it rest often upon very unsubstantial foundations. The reason is simply that pictorial art is not articulate in the same degree as literature. If the story is known, the meaning of the illustration is obvious, but to reconstruct the story from the illustration is not lightly to be attempted with any confidence in the accuracy of the result. Suppose that Macaulay's New Zealander possessed the whole series of the illustrations to *Alice in Wonderland*, it is not very probable that his reconstruction would at all closely correspond to the original, even if he knew the order in which the pictures should be arranged.

Of course, I do not wish to deny all value to this kind of evidence. The discoveries of Mycenaean works of art depicting a woman riding on a bull, or a monster of Chimaera form, do strengthen the argument that the stories of Europa and Bellerophon *may* have been known in the Mycenaean Age. But they do not prove more. We cannot be certain that a woman riding on a bull is necessarily an illustration of Europa's adventure or that a Chimaera-like monster certainly implies that his creator knew the tale of Bellerophon. Miss Harrison once drew very startling and far-reaching conclusions from a well-known and beautiful vase depicting Athena standing in front of a large dragon from whose jaws hangs the limp body of a dead man; on a tree behind hangs the skin or dead body of a ram.[1] She may, of course, be right that we have here an unrecorded and strangely different version of the story of Jason, but there are no names on the design to indicate the characters. Athena and the corpse are both inappro-

[1] J. E. Harrison, *Themis*, p. 436.

83   6-2

priate in the Argonaut story, though it is true enough
that a dragon and a fleece would fit in well. The truth is
that we do not know what the vase does illustrate.

The real value of vase paintings lies in the fact that
names are often attached by the painters to the figures,
and, further, that the scenes depicted and thus certified
sometimes establish the currency of characteristic
details at an earlier date than any literary record. An
example is the vase depicting Perseus killing the sea
monster by the hurling of stones (see below, p. 122).

CHAPTER V

PROCNE AND PHILOMELA

The tale of Procne and Philomela is deservedly among the most famous in European literature and among those best beloved by our English poets. It is concerned primarily with four birds, the nightingale, the swallow, the hawk and the hoopoe. The hoopoe, as we shall see, came into it because it was mistakenly considered to be a metamorphosed hawk. The stories explain why it is that the hawk pursues the nightingale and the swallow and account at the same time for certain characteristics attributed to the songs and habits of these latter birds.

Both the nightingale[1] and the swallow[2] appear in spring. "When the hillside is already bushy" (ὅταν τὸ ὄρος ἤδη δασύνηται) the nightingale sings, so Aristotle tells us, for fifteen days and nights continuously: afterwards its song is not continuous and finally it ceases.[3] In Attica it arrives towards the end of March or the beginning of April[4] and it is as the harbinger of spring that Electra calls it Διὸς ἄγγελος.[5] Popular rhymes in England and in Germany attest its supposed

---

[1] For Greek beliefs about the nightingale see D'Arcy Thompson, *A Glossary of Greek Birds*, pp. 10–14.
[2] For Greek beliefs about the swallow see D'Arcy Thompson, *op. cit.* pp. 186–192.
[3] Aristotle, *Hist. An.* ix, 49 B, 633 b.
[4] For the facts see Jebb, *Oedipus Coloneus*, p. xii.
[5] Sophocles, *Electra*, 149.

arrival upon April 14th,[1] when "longen folk to goon on pilgrimages".[2]

The swallow is even more notoriously the harbinger of spring and summer.[3] The scene of the arrival of the first swallow is delightfully depicted upon a well-known black-figured vase in the Vatican;[4] the Swallow Song of ancient Rhodes has its counterparts in modern Greece,[5] and Swainson has quoted abundant evidence for its popular character in Europe as the bringer of spring or summer.

"The fable", says Pausanias of Procne and Philomela, "that they were turned into nightingale and swallow was suggested I suppose by the plaintive and dirge-like song of these birds."[6] Swallow and nightingale are associated as birds of spring, but this further association as birds of dirge-like song is at first sight surprising,[7]

[1]   "On the third of April (o.s.)
          Come in cuckoo and nightingale."
       "Tiburtius kommt mit Ruf und Schall,
          Er bringt den Kukuk und die Nachtigal."
       "Wenn Maximus tritt in die Hall
          So bringt er uns die Nachtigal."
                  Swainson, *The Folk-lore of British Birds*, p. 19.
[2]   "the smale fowles maken melodye
          that sleepen al the night with open eye."
                  Chaucer, *Canterbury Tales, Prologue*, 9.
[3] E.g. Simonides, *fr.* 74; Aristophanes, *Birds*, 714; *Thesmoph.* 1; *Frag.* 499; Schol. Aristoph. *Birds*, 39.
[4] Baumeister, *Denkmäler des Alterthums*, iii, Fig. 2128; reproduced also in J. E. Harrison, *Themis*, p. 8.
[5] See Halliday, *Folk-lore Studies*, pp. 120 f. Texts of modern Greek "swallow songs" in Passow, *Popularia carmina Graeciae recentioris*, Nos. 305–309.
[6] Pausanias, i, 41, 9.
[7] Ancient taste in bird song was different from ours. We should not choose the lark as an example of cacophony or say "if a lark can sing like a swan and if owls dare compete with nightingales, if a

though we shall see that the ancient Greeks were not
alone in attributing a sinister aspect to the swallow. The
sweet melancholy of the nightingale's song, it is true, no
modern poet would question. It certainly impressed
with its sadness[1] the ancient Greek ear, which heard in
its reiterated note a sound like Itys, Aitylus or Itylus.[2]
This word may well mean "a tender youth", but it is
none the less onomatopoeic.[3] The ancients were also
inevitably impressed by the fact that unlike most birds it
sang after sundown. This characteristic, which has given
the bird its name in English and German, gave rise to
the belief among the ancients that it never slept.[4] In
Chaucer's *Prologue* it is said of the Squyer that

> So hote he lovede that by nighte tale
> He sleep namore than dooth a nightingale.[5]

cuckoo asserts he is more sweet-voiced than a cicada, then I too
can equal Palladius", *Anth. Pal.* ix, 380.

[1] οἰκτρᾶς γόον ὄρνιθος ἀηδοῦς, Sophocles, *Ajax*, 628. Cf.
Sophocles, *Electra*, 107; Euripides, *Rhesus*, 550.

[2] Ἴτυν, Ἴτυν στένουσα. Aeschylus, *Agamemnon*, 1144.
ἀλλ' ἐμέ γ' ἁ στονόεσσ' ἄραρεν φρένας,
ἃ Ἴτυν, αἰὲν Ἴτυν ὀλοφύρεται
ὄρνις ἀτυζομένα. Sophocles, *Electra*, 147.

[3] Roscher, in Roscher, *Lexikon*, s.v. Aedon, followed by Miss
Harrison, *J.H.S.* viii, p. 442, denies that Itys is onomatopoeic, but
compare the "Taille vite" of the story quoted below or the
Westphalian story in which the nightingale's note becomes "Is tit,
is tit, to wit, to wit—Trizy, Trizy, to bucht, to bucht, to bucht",
Swainson, *op. cit.* p. 21.

[4] τᾶμος ἄυπνος κλυτὸς ὄρθρος ἐγείρησιν ἀηδόνας, Ibycus,
Frag. 7. Cf. Aelian, *Var. Hist.* xii, 20 = Hesiod (Rzach), *Frag.*
203, which is quoted below, p. 89, note 2. Possibly this is in
Sophocles' mind in the comparison of Deianeira, sleepless from
grief, to a sorrowing bird, Sophocles, *Trachiniae*, 105.

[5] Chaucer, *Canterbury Tales*, *Prologue*, 97. Cf. line 9 quoted
above, p. 86, n. 2.

But this comparison need not be due to Chaucer's knowledge of the classics, for the sleeplessness of the nightingale is a commonplace of European folk-lore, though a variety of reasons are offered to account for the phenomenon. The truth of the belief alluded to by Shakespeare,

> And whiles against a thorn thou bearest thy part
> To keep thy sharp woes waking,[1]

is questioned by Sir Thomas Browne,[2] who is concerned, however, with the nightingale's dread of the serpent, which both in France and England is frequently alleged to be the cause of the bird's adopting this means to keep awake. In the Franche Comté it is explained that the nightingale never sleeps when the vines begin to shoot until the tendrils are dressed, because it fears to be snared by them, and that the sound, which the Greeks rendered Itys, is "Taille vite", addressed to the vine-dresser.[3] Another French story explains how the nightingale borrowed the blindworm's eye and keeps awake in order to prevent the blindworm from getting it back. In Westphalia, the nightingale was once a shepherdess who incessantly postponed marriage, until her lover cursed her with sleeplessness until the Day of Judgment. This very general belief in the sleeplessness of the bird explains why its eyes and heart, if dissolved and secretly administered to anyone in drink, "he will

[1] Shakespeare, *Lucrece*, stanzas 162–164.
[2] Sir Thomas Browne, *Pseudodoxia*, iii, 28.
[3] Swainson, *op. cit.* p. 21.

never sleep, but will so die, and it admits not of cure".[1]

The swallow, according to Aelian,[2] was awake half the night; but to this belief I know of no parallel, and it would seem to be derived directly from the association of the two birds in our story. Both ancients and moderns have recognised the swallow's domestic associations; its habit of nesting under the eaves or in the rafters has given it the character of the friend of man,[3] and some ancient poets have testified to the sweetness of its song.[4] In spite of this, however, the swallow in folk-lore has a dual character, and a sinister aspect has been attributed to it in popular belief. In Ireland, it is regarded as the devil's bird; in Caithness, as a witch hag; in France, a swallow flying under the belly of a cow will turn its milk to blood; in England, its presence sometimes portends

[1] Swainson, *op. cit.* pp. 20, 21. A variant to the vineyard story from Toulouse attributes the nightingale's wakefulness to dread of being caught by the tendrils of "Virgin's Seal" (*tamnus communis*).

[2] Aelian, *Var. Hist.* xii, 20 = Hesiod (Rzach), *Frag.* 203: λέγει Ἡσίοδος τὴν ἀηδόνα μόνην ὀρνίθων ἀμοιρεῖν ὕπνου καὶ διὰ τέλους ἀγρυπνεῖν· τὴν δὲ χελιδόνα οὐκ ἐς τὸ παντελὲς ἀγρυπνεῖν, ἀποβεβληκέναι δὲ καὶ ταύτην τοῦ ὕπνου τὸ ἥμισυ. τιμωρίαν δὲ ἄρα ταύτην ἐκτίνουσι διὰ τὸ πάθος τὸ ἐν Θρᾴκῃ κατατολμηθὲν τὸ ἐς τὸ δεῖπνον ἐκεῖνο τὸ ἄθεσμον. The last sentence is clearly an addition of Aelian. It is not safe evidence that the version of serving up Itys was known to Hesiod. On the other hand, if Aelian is right that Hesiod mentioned the partial sleeplessness of the swallow, it is from the association of the nightingale and swallow in the Itys story that the alleged characteristic must be derived.

[3] Aelian, *Nat. An.* x, 34; Artemidorus, *On.* iv, 58. See also the passages collected by Frazer in *Classical Review*, v, 1891, pp. 1-3.

[4] E.g. ἀδυμελὲς χαρίεσσα χελιδοῖ, Anacreon, 67.

death.[1] If we turn to the ancient world we shall find a good deal of evidence for the ill-omened character of the swallow and particularly of its twittering. The swallow is linked with the nightingale in the *Lament for Bion*[2] as a singer of sad lament; Hesychius agrees with Pausanias that its song is a dirge;[3] it was in the form of a swallow that Isis, in the Greek version of her history, flew round the sacred post bemoaning her misfortune and sad fate.[4] "O daughter of Pandion with the plaintive twittering voice...why dost thou complain, swallow, all day in the house?" writes a poet in the *Anthology*.[5] The precept of the Pythagoreans that no swallow should be allowed to enter the house was doubtless founded, like the other Pythagorean taboos, upon a popular superstition,[6] and Artemidorus by attempting to controvert it bears witness to the general view that the swallow's cry was of mournful import.[7] One reason

---

[1] See references in Frazer, *loc. cit.*; Swainson, *op. cit.* p. 54; Henderson, *Folk-lore of the Northern Counties of England and the Borders*, pp. 48, 123.

[2]   οὐδὲ τόσον ποκ' ἄεισεν ἐνὶ σκοπέλοισιν ἀηδών,
    οὐδὲ τόσον θρήνησεν ἀν' ὤρεα μακρὰ χελιδών.
                          [Moschus, iii], 38.
For the swallow and nightingale as sweet singers, Alcaeus, *fr.* 3: ἄδουσι μὲν ἀηδόνες αὐτῷ, ἄδουσι δὲ καὶ χελιδόνες. Cf. Lucian, *Ver. Hist.* ii, 15; *Philopatris*, 3; Longinus, *Past.* ii, 3.

[3] Hesychius, s.v. πύθου χελιδόνος· παροιμιῶδες, διότι ὀδυρτικὸν τὸ ζῶον· θρηνεῖ γὰρ ἡ χελιδών.

[4] Plutarch, *Is. et Os.* 16, p. 357 c.

[5] Mnasalcas in *Anth. Pal.* ix, 70. Cf. ix. 57.

[6] Plutarch, *Quaest. Conuiu.* viii, 7; Diog. Laert. viii, 17; Clem. Alex. *Strom.* v, 5. A very general explanation was that it implied a symbolic prohibition of malicious backbiting and chatter.

[7] Artemidorus, *On.* ii, 71. The swallow's song, it is claimed, is not mournful but hortatory.

perhaps that the swallow's twittering was regarded as ill-omened was that to Greek ears it has the sinister quality of savage half-human speech. "Cleophon upon whose double-speaking lips the Thracian swallow is terribly roaring as she sits upon the barbarian leafage and sings her tearful nightingale's lament."[1] The swallow's cry not only sounded mournful to the Greeks, but also like human speech mutilated either by physical injury or by the inarticulateness of a barbarous unintelligible language.[2] Hence the jargon of the Thracian Triballos in the *Birds* of Aristophanes is likened by Poseidon to the swallow's twittering.[3]

So much for the nightingale and the swallow; the hawk comes into the story solely as the pursuer of small birds. His place was taken by the hoopoe in the fifth century B.C., and the justification for the substitution was no doubt the popular belief that the hoopoe was but the hawk in another form. The hoopoe, like the nightingale and the swallow, is a spring to autumn migrant in

[1] ...Κλεοφῶντος ἐφ' οὗ δὴ χείλεσιν ἀμφιλάλοις δεινὸν ἐπι-
βρέμεται
Θρηκία χελιδὼν
ἐπὶ βάρβαρον ἑζομένη πέταλον·
κελαδεῖ δ' ἐπίκλαυτον ἀηδόνιον νόμον, ὡς ἀπολεῖται κἂν ἴσαι
γένωνται.   Aristophanes, *Frogs*, 678–685.
Note again the close association of the songs of the swallow and nightingale.

[2]   ἀλλ' εἴπερ ἐστὶ μὴ χελιδόνος δίκην
          ἀγνῶτα φωνὴν βάρβαρον κεκτημένη,
          ἔσω φρενῶν λέγουσα πείθω νιν λόγῳ.
                              Aeschylus, *Agam.* 1050.
Hesychius, χελιδόσι· τοὺς βαρβάρους χελιδόσιν ἀπεικάζουσι διὰ τὴν ἀσύνθετον λαλιάν.

[3] Aristophanes, *Birds*, 1681 and Schol.

Greece, though it breeds in Macedonia and perhaps in Epirus,[1] and I find it difficult to credit Oder's contention that it first appeared in Attica in the fifth century B.C. and was a rare and novel bird at the time when Sophocles wrote his play.[2] It is in reality a shy and timid little bird frequenting desert places, a habit which lends verisimilitude to the theory that it is under a curse or remorseful for some unforgettable crime. In spite, however, of its timidity, its bright colouring and crested helmet have given it in popular belief the dignity of a bird of war,[3] and it was no doubt this martial appearance which inspired the belief that, like another migrant, the cuckoo, in ancient and modern superstition,[4] the hoopoe, which in Bavaria is known as the cuckoo's lackey,[5] was a metamorphosed hawk.[6] The sudden appearance of a migrant is thus accounted for by supposing that it is a non-migrant undergoing a seasonal change of form.[7]

[1] D'Arcy Thompson, *op. cit.* p. 55.

[2] Oder, "Der Wiedehopf in der griechischen Saga", *Rhein. Mus.* N.F. xliii, 1888, pp. 540 f.

[3] Pausanias, x, 4, 8, with Frazer's note *ad loc.*; Aristophanes, *Birds*, 94, 279; Ovid, *Met.* vi, 672 f. For the hoopoe in Swedish folk-lore as an army bird which foretells war see Swainson, *op. cit.* p. 106.

[4] Swainson, *op. cit.* p. 113.

[5] Swainson, *op. cit.* p. 109.

[6] Aristotle, *Hist. An.* ix, 15, 616; 49, 633. Aristotle ostensibly quotes Aeschylus, and Pliny, *N.H.* x, 86, has copied from Aristotle. It is practically certain, however, that Aeschylus is a mistake for Sophocles. See Sophocles, *Frag.* 581 (Pearson-Jebb) and Pearson's notes *ad loc.*

[7] An analogous result of misunderstanding of the facts of migration is the superstition that swallows hibernate; see Halliday, *Greek Divination*, p. 260.

With the scatological reputation of the hoopoe in ancient and modern folk-lore we are not here concerned, nor with the knowledge which it shares with the woodpecker and the swallow of the magical herb which opens locks;[1] some of its characteristics, however, were appropriate to its inclusion in a story which provided for them an explanation. In most languages the name of the bird (Greek epops, Latin upupa, French huppe, and English hoopoe) has been derived from its cry.[2] This sounded to the Greeks as ποῦ, ποῦ,[3] and indicated an endless and unsuccessful search. This theory is reinforced by the antics of the bird. "Like the lapwing it has the credit of being able to point out the locality of hidden springs. This idea seems to have arisen from the habit of the bird, when settling on the ground, of bending down the head and raising it suddenly with a jerky motion."[4] Hence "in this military shape he is aptly phancied even still revengefully to pursue his hated wife Progne; in the propriety of his Note crying *Pou, Pou, Ubi, Ubi*, or *Where are you?*"[5] Further, we may note that though

[1] See D'Arcy Thompson, *op. cit.* pp. 54–57; Swainson, *op. cit.* pp. 106–107.
[2] Similarly the hoopoe in Grimm, *Kinder- und Hausmärchen*, 173, calls *Up, up*.
[3] Eustathius *ad* Homer, *Odyssey*, xix, 518; Tzetzes, *Chil.* vii, 479.
[4] Swainson, *op. cit.* p. 107. Swainson has missed the fact that the lapwing is consequently sometimes confused with the hoopoe. "We are little obliged unto our School instruction, wherein we are taught to render *Upupa* a Lapwing," Sir Thomas Browne, *An Answer to Certain Queries relating to Fishes, Birds and Beasts*, Tract iv.
[5] Sir Thomas Browne, *loc. cit.*

the name epops is derived onomatopoeically from the hoopoe's cry, it has a good meaning of its own, and that meaning is synonymous with Tereus.[1] Here, perhaps, is one reason why Tereus became a hoopoe.

Let us turn now to the stories which were woven to account for the supposed characteristics of these birds. The simplest and the earliest version is concerned with the nightingale alone, and explains the lovely melancholy of her song as due to the unending grief of a mother who slew her child unwittingly. In *Odyssey*, xix, 518 f., Penelope compares herself to the nightingale. "Even as when the daughter of Pandareus, the nightingale of the greensward, sings sweet in the first season of the spring, from her place in the thick leafage of the trees, and with many a turn and trill she pours forth her full-voiced music bewailing her child, dear Itylus, whom once on a time she slew with the sword unwittingly, Itylus the son of Zethus the prince; even as her song my troubled soul sways to and fro." This version appears to be alluded to by Pausanias, ix, 5, 9, who tells us that Zethus died of grief, and it is depicted upon a red-figured Panaetius vase, where Aedon is seen to be slaying Itys with a sword.[2]

It is tantalising that for the details of this story we are

---

[1] Hesychius, s.v. ἔποψ· ἐπόπτης, δυνάστης καὶ εἶδος ὀρνέου. τοῦτον δ' ἐπόπτην ἔοπα τῶν αὑτοῦ κακῶν, Sophocles, *Frag.* 581 (Pearson-Jebb), with which compare ὁ Τηρεὺς...ὄρνις γίνεται· καὶ τηροῦσι ἔτι τοῦ πάθους τὴν εἰκόνα, Achilles Tatius, v, 5. Cf. Schol. Aristoph. *Birds*, 102, ὁ λεγόμενος Τηρεὺς παρὰ τὸ τηρεῖν τὴν Ἰώ, and *Et. Mag.* 757, 45.

[2] J. E. Harrison, "Itys and Aedon: a Panaitios cylix", *J.H.S.* viii, 1887, p. 439.

necessarily dependent upon late commentators.[1] From
them two versions emerge, but of these we may perhaps
dispose of one out of hand. Thrämer, it is true, regards
it as a genuinely early and local variant, and labels it
"the West Greek version";[2] but it bears all the marks
of Alexandrine invention, and I suspect that it had its
origin in the attempt to bolster up the alternative reading
of Zetes for Zethus in the Homeric text adopted by some
ancient scholar who shared Thrämer's astonishment at
Aedon's appearance in Theban story.[3] The version was
known to Eustathius, on the authority of "an ancient
document", as well as to Helladius, the Byzantine lexicographer from whom Suidas and Photius drew much of
their material. According to this version, Aedon was
the daughter of Pandareus of Dulichium, who married
Zetes the Boread, by whom she had a son Aitylus. She
suspected her husband of an intrigue with a Hamadryad
and that he was therein abetted by her son. In revenge
she slew Aitylus, but repenting her crime, she, who was
once a woman but is now a bird, laments her son,
finding no respite from her deed of horror. Even
Thrämer confesses that the etymological connection be-
tween Zetes = $Za\acute{\eta}\tau\eta s$ and $"H\tau v\lambda os$ = $'A\acute{\eta}\tau v\lambda os$, which
Eustathius mentions, "has the appearance of etymolo-

[1] Scholia and Eustathius *ad* Homer, *Odyssey*, xix, 518; Photius,
Bib. p. 531 (Bekker).
[2] Thrämer in Pauly-Wissowa, i, pp. 467 f., s.v. *Aedon*.
[3] "Vermutlich ist nur der Namensanklang von Zetes an Zethos
die Veranlassung gewesen Aedon in das Bereich der thebanischen
Herrensage hineinzuziehen." Thus Thrämer, but it is far more
probable that Zetes is an unintelligent emendation of Zethus. The
Aedon story falls within a group of Boeotian-Anatolian legends.

95

gising arbitrariness". The intrigue with the Hamadryad stamps the version as not earlier than Hellenistic. The whole thing appears to be a learned invention necessitated by the initial substitution of Zetes for Zethus, and Eustathius seems to have found for it a happy word, ἐρεσχελία, "much ado about nothing".

The other version appears to go back in the main to Pherecydes.[1] Aedon, daughter of Pandareus of Miletus, married Zethus of Thebes, by whom she had two children, Itylus and Neïs, the latter being the eponym of the Neïtan Gate of Thebes. She was jealous of her sister-in-law, who had six children to her two,[2] and consequently plotted to kill her eldest nephew, Alalcomeneus or Amaleus. But in one version the nightcaps, in another the positions of the children in the bed, had been changed, and Aedon consequently killed her own son Itylus by mistake. Hence as a bird she continues to lament the death of Itylus.

That this, the earliest recorded form of the story of Aedon, is localised at Thebes need cause us no surprise. Zethus marries the daughter of Pandareus of Miletus, while his brother marries Niobe, the daughter of Tantalus, and the story of their magical building of the walls of Thebes shows affinity with the story of the building of

---

[1] Jacoby, *Fr. Hist. Gr.* Pherecydes, *frags.* 124, 125, 126. Scholia and Eustathius *ad* Homer, *Odyssey*, xix, 518. Eustathius has the changing of the positions of the children in the bed, which probably but not explicitly derives from Pherecydes.

[2] There is a slip here. Pherecydes gave the number of Niobe's children as six of either sex; on the other hand παῖδας cannot here mean boys, for Neïs was a girl and Aedon had but one boy. At some stage there has been a *lapsus calami*.

96

the walls of Troy. Our tale, in fact, belongs to a group of legendary contacts between Boeotia and Ionia, some of which I have discussed elsewhere.[1] They are due primarily, I believe, to the prominent part played in the settlement of Ionia by the noble houses of Boeotia. Whether the form of the tale which Pherecydes gives would have been known to the author of the *Iliad* I should be inclined to doubt, though the Ionian reactions upon Boeotian saga are undoubtedly very early. In this connection it would be interesting to know whether the sister-in-law of Aedon in the *Odyssey* was Hippomedusa or Niobe.

Before leaving this earliest explanation of the nightingale's sad song, we may notice that the tragic mistake by which the wrong child is murdered is an incident which in various forms occurs with frequency in Indo-European folk-tale.[2] When the ogress comes to kill the band of brothers or sisters who are sleeping in her house, the clever brother or sister has changed their positions, nightcaps or other distinguishing marks, and in the dark the ogress slays her own offspring by mistake. A similar episode occurred in the plot of Euripides' *Ino*, in which Themisto arranged for her own children to wear white night-clothes and those of Ino dark. But Ino changed the night-clothes and so Themisto killed her own children by mistake.[3]

It is probable that a story in which the nightingale

[1] Halliday, *Annals of Archaeology and Anthropology*, xi, pp. 11 f.
[2] See the references in Bolte and Polívka, *Anmerkungen zu den Kinder- und Hausmärchen der Brüder Grimm*, i, pp. 124, 499 f.
[3] See Robert, *Griechische Heldensage*, p. 49.

and the swallow were associated in a common tragedy was known to Hesiod,[1] who certainly knew that the swallow was the daughter of Pandion.[2] Sappho, too, alludes to Chelidon as the daughter of Pandion.[3] The first quite certain evidence, however, of a story in which Aedon and Chelidon were joint heroines is a metope from Aetolian Thermum belonging to the late seventh or early sixth century B.C.[4] In the next literary reference Tereus is mentioned, and the story evidently includes the metamorphosis of the husband into a hawk and explains the hawk's pursuit of the songbirds. The Chorus in the *Supplices* of Aeschylus speaks of the lament of Tereus' wife, the hawk-chased nightingale, who weaves in song the story of her own child's death, how he met with an unnatural mother's wrath and perished by murder at her hand.[5] The heroines are probably still Aedon and Chelidon, and Tereus is a hawk, but the murder is evidently deliberate, not committed upon her own child by mistake for another. In fact it would seem that in its main outlines the story, later familiar, had taken shape by the time of Aeschylus. But the canonical form of the story was clearly fixed by the *Tereus* of Sophocles, the

[1] Hesiod (Rzach), *Frag.* 203; see p. 89, n. 2, above.
[2] Hesiod, *Op. et Di.* 568:

τὸν δὲ μέτ' ὀρθογόη Πανδιονὶς ὦρτο Χελιδὼν
ἐς φάος ἀνθρώποις ἔαρος νέον ἱσταμένοιο.

'Then is the time to prune your vines': compare the French story of the nightingale who sings "Taille vite", p. 88, above.
[3] Sappho, *Frag.* 88: τί με Πανδιονὶς ὦ᾽ραννα Χελιδών.
[4] Robert, *Griechische Heldensage*, p. 155; *Ant. Denkmäler*, ii, Taf. 50, 1. One sister is labelled ΧΕΛΣΔFON; the first A of Aedon is preserved.   [5] Aeschylus, *Supplices*, 58 f.

98

plot of which is fairly easily established in its main lines from the surviving fragments and the comments of later writers.[1]

The scene was set in Thrace. Tereus, the king of Thrace, in recognition of assistance rendered to the Athenian king in war, had been given to wife Procne, the daughter of Pandion, king of Athens. Lonely in her husband's savage home, Procne suggested a visit from her sister Philomela and besought Tereus to go to Athens to fetch her. Tereus became enamoured of Philomela and on the journey violated her. To conceal his crime he cut out Philomela's tongue and gave out that she was dead. Philomela, however, wove the story of the crime upon an embroidered robe which she found means to convey to Procne. The sisters met and plotted revenge. They slew Itys, Procne's son by Tereus, and served up his flesh to Tereus. When the feast was over they revealed to the father the nature of the dish: rising in horror he upset the table and pursued the sisters to slay them. But the gods turned them all into birds, Procne into a nightingale, Philomela into a swallow and Tereus into a hoopoe. Hence the hoopoe perpetually pursues the nightingale and the swallow; the nightingale continually laments her son Itys, while the twittering swallow for ever attempts to tell her tale in vain, since the brutal ravisher had torn out her tongue and made her inarticulate.

That Sophocles' play aroused great interest is shown by the polemic of Thucydides on the question of the scene

[1] Pearson-Jebb, *The Fragments of Sophocles*, ii, pp. 221–228.

of the tragedy, to which we must return when we discuss the problem of Tereus and the Thracians, and by the *Birds* of Aristophanes, in which the hoopoe is king of Cloud-cuckoo-land and more than one allusion is made to the play of the tragedian. Sophocles seems certainly to have been the first poet to adopt the substitution of hoopoe for hawk, though this change undoubtedly has its origin in the popular superstition, which Sophocles did not invent, that in the spring some hawks turned into hoopoes. Sophocles, too, seems to have been the first to give personal names to Aedon and Chelidon. I think that we may agree with Robert that these are simply proper names.[1] Attempts have been made to make them appropriate to the birds. Some have connected Procne with περκνός, "the dark or tawny nightingale", and others have relied upon the sweetness of πρόκνις, a sort of candied fig, though, as Robert points out, the derivation, if correct, gives a name appropriate rather to a "sweet maid" than to a sweet singer. Philomela has been explained as having its origin in the swallow's habit of nesting in the sheep stalls: a far-fetched hypothesis, for μῆλα means sheep and not their stalls, and swallows nest in houses, not in Greek sheep stalls, which are not in fact like stables. Another derivation, canonised in the eighth edition of Liddell and Scott but certainly wrong, is that Philomela means "song loving", the ε of μέλος having been lengthened into η. Philomela, however, would seem simply to mean "lover of sheep". It is a good heroic feminine name,

[1] Robert, *Griechische Heldensage*, p. 156.

witness Philomela the daughter of Actor.[1] The attractive theory then that Procne and Philomela were popular names for the nightingale and the swallow, like the animal nicknames in Hesiod,[2] can hardly be entertained. They are probably just personal names, and for the purposes of this story the invention of Sophocles.

In any case, ever since the production of the *Tereus* these proper names have been permanently attached to the heroines of the story, though a curious inversion subsequently took place. That the variation was possible was due no doubt to the fact that they were but proper names of uncertain significance and consequently transferable in a way in which Aedon and Chelidon were not. The mistaken etymology Philomela, "lover of song", may have helped. At any rate the name Philomela was transferred to Aedon and Chelidon became Procne, probably in some subsequent tragedy, perhaps a play of Carcinus. Through the Hellenistic writers this new nomenclature passed to the Romans and so to the English poets.[3] The mythographers who did not make the con-

[1] Schol. Ap. Rhod. iv, 816 (*F.H.G.* iv, 505); Eustathius, *Il.* 1053, 52.

[2] E.g. φερέοικος, "snail", Hesiod, *Op. et Di.* 571; ἄτριχος, "snake", *Frag.* 96.

[3] The Latin writers generally made Philomela the nightingale and Procne the swallow. Many of them made the consequential alteration that Philomela was the wife and Procne the ravished sister. But not all mythographers thus avoided making the nightingale tongueless by this second adjustment. See Conington's note to Virgil, *Ec.* vi, 78. It is hardly necessary to attest the English usage:

> And the mute silence hist along,
> 'Less Philomel will deign a song
> In her sweetest, saddest plight,
> Smoothing the rugged brow of night.

sequential alteration and give Philomela the nightingale
to Tereus for his bride were responsible for the curious
medieval superstition that nightingales had no tongues,
anent which there is an entertaining passage in Sir
Thomas Browne: "Franciscus Sanctus in a laudable
comment upon Alcat's Emblems affirmeth, and that
from experience, a Nightingale hath no tongue. Avem
Philomelam lingua carere pro certo affirmare possum,
nisi me oculi fallunt. Which if any man for a while shall
believe upon his experience, he may at his leisure refute
it by his own".[1]

Of the other features in the Sophoclean version, the
bride's loneliness in a savage husband's country and her
desire for a visit from her sister, or alternatively her
longing to revisit her home, are commonplaces of fairy
tale.[2] The method of revealing a story through weaving
a picture or a message upon a robe or carpet is also a
common episode in *märchen*, though it is interesting to
notice that it is more frequent and more popular in
Eastern than in Western stories. A special form of it is
connected with the injunction upon Ottoman sultans
to learn the practice of a handicraft. The incident of
serving up Itys to his father for food is a new feature in
the story, but, though Greek in origin, it is borrowed.
The model from which it derives is undoubtedly the
tale of Lycaon and the sacrilegious meal which he
offered to Zeus. In Ovid's version even the detail is

---

[1] Sir Thomas Browne, *Pseudodoxia*, i, p. vii.
[2] E.g. Psyche's longing to see her sisters and assuage their grief
in Apuleius, *Met.* v, 5 f., or the converse in Grimm, No. 91.

imitated, for the overturned table, unmotivated here, has its special point in the Arcadian original, in which it accounts for the place-name Trapezus.[1] That the story of Lycaon, connected as it undoubtedly is with some form of human sacrifice which seems to have persisted up to the time of Pausanias, is an hieratic legend connected with the savage ritual of Lycaean Zeus, appears to me almost certain. The story of the serving up of Pelops by Tantalus may also have had a ritual origin and have been in the first place connected with some rite of human sacrifice and sacrament. In the Banquet of Thyestes the hieratic legend would appear to have been secularised and used to provide a sensational episode. It is similarly used here in the story of Tereus, in the story of Harpalyce and Clymenus,[2] not probably a very early or genuine tradition, and in a slightly different form in the quite artificial katasterismic story of Matusius, Demophon and his daughters.[3] It is finally turned to account in secular history in the tale of the punishment of Harpagus by Astyages on account of his sparing the life of Cyrus.[4] As a minor confirmation of the Greek source of this latter legend we may notice that a detail of the Banquet of Thyestes, to which Professor Murray draws special attention and from which he draws some more than hazardous conclusions,[5] recurs

---

[1] See Halliday, *The Greek Questions of Plutarch*, p. 170.
[2] Parthenius, *Narr. Am.* xiii; Hyginus, *Fab.* 206.
[3] Phylarchus, *Frag.* 83 (Müller, *F.H.G.* vol. i); *Frag.* 69 (Jacoby, vol. ii) = Hyginus, *Poet. astron.* ii, 40, 413.
[4] Herodotus, i, 107–119.
[5] Murray in *Anthropology and the Classics*, p. 73.

in this piece of Persian history. When Harpagus has eaten, the head and feet of his son are produced and shown to him.

We must turn now to the villain of the piece, Tereus. The Aedon story was localised at Thebes, but Chelidon as early as Hesiod was recognised as the daughter of Pandion. The combination of the two birds in one story does in fact seem to have brought the tale into the area of Attic legend. Now Tereus appears originally to have been a Megarian hero. The Megarians alleged that he was an early king of Pagae, and in the Megarid there was a definite cult of Tereus of which a very peculiar and probably very ancient feature was the use of gravel instead of barley grain at the annual sacrifice.[1] Now at an early date Megarian and Attic legend became considerably intertwined, and confusion has been increased by the fact that legendary connections were exploited for political purposes. It is precisely in this nexus of Attic-Megarian legend that Pandion II, who is reckoned by Pausanias to be the father of Procne, has his importance. The story of the partition of his dominions among his sons was probably invented at the court of Pisistratus. In this Nisus, a son of Pandion, surrendered his claim to Attica to his brother Aegeus. According to Attic tradition Nisus himself was buried in Athens; even the Megarians admitted him to be a son of the exiled Pandion by a daughter of Pylas, king of Megara.[2] In the first place, therefore, I suspect that

[1] Pausanias, i, 41, 6.
[2] See Halliday, *The Greek Questions of Plutarch*, pp. 92 f.

Tereus was simply a Megarian hero who came into the story through Pandion II's connection with Megarian saga. The notorious sharp sight of the hawk may have made his name appropriate for the husband and pursuer of the nightingale. But by the fifth century B.C. everyone was agreed that Tereus was a Thracian, though it was hotly debated whether he was a real Thracian from Thrace or one of the Thracians who were alleged once to have inhabited Phocis. There were perhaps two reasons why Tereus should become a Thracian. One is the savage character of the story, which at any rate in the fifth century seemed more appropriately attributed to a "barbarian"; and, even among barbarians, Thracians were notorious for their savagery and disregard of human life.[1] The second reason is the similarity between the sound of Tereus and that of the Thracian name Teres, which leads Thucydides to open his account of the contemporary Thracian monarch by explaining that the reader must not confuse Teres of Thrace with Tereus the husband of Procne.[2] I should myself, however, be inclined to doubt whether Tereus was thought to be a Thracian king much before the fifth century. There is nothing, of course, in the mythographers making him a son of Ares.[3] Ares is a Thracian, and he is also an appropriate father for a monster of inhumanity.

[1] Not undeservedly; witness the unprovoked assault by the Thracian mercenaries on Mycalessus and the slaughter of the children at school. Thucydides, vii, 29.

[2] Thucydides, ii, 29.

[3] E.g. Apollodorus, iii, 14, 8; Hyginus, *Fab.* 45; Ovid, *Met.* vi, 427.

But a small point, consistent in the tradition, seems to me definitely to belong to the period when Thracian military help, whether by alliance or by hire of mercenaries, was becoming important in the Greek world. According to Apollodorus and others, it was on account of military assistance against Labdacus that Tereus received Procne's hand as a reward from Pandion, and Thucydides leaves no doubt that in the tradition, which he knew, it was undisputed that Tereus had lent military aid to Pandion.

The passage in Thucydides is a polemic, presumably directed against Sophocles. Tereus was a Thracian, but not an Odrysian Thracian: he was king of Daulis in what is now known as Phocis, which was then inhabited by Thracians, and it was there that the Itys episode occurred. The evidence is that many poets call the nightingale "the Daulian bird", while it is much more probable that Pandion would have made a marriage alliance with a king in Phocis than with one in remote Thrace. Well, of course, it is true that poets before Thucydides and since have spoken of the Daulian bird, but the name Daulis itself is derived from $\delta a \hat{v} \lambda o s$, "a thicket": "the bird of the thicket" would be appropriate to Homer's Aedon, who "sings sweet in the first season of the spring, from her place in the thick leafage of the trees", or, as Aristotle puts it, $\ddot{o}\tau a\nu$ $\tau\dot{o}$ $\ddot{o}\rho os$ $\ddot{\eta}\delta\eta$ $\delta a\sigma\dot{v}\nu\eta\tau a\iota$. Actually, too, the thickets of Daulis abound in nightingales: Pausanias' (x, 4, 9) improvement of the evidence for the localisation of the story that no swallow will nest there is simply a fiction, for swallows also there abound.[1] I see no evidence whatever for the specifically local version of the legend peculiar to Daulis, which scholars declare to exist without expounding its content. Daulis was "a well nightingaled vicinity": either from this, or perhaps originally by a direct derivation from δαῦλος, the nightingale was called the Daulian bird. There was a theory among ancient scholars, which some moderns would take more seriously than I should be prepared to do, that the pre-Greek population of Phocis was Thracian. The reasons why the affair should have happened at Daulis are then obvious, and this localisation pleasantly rounds the argument in a circle that Thracians once inhabited Phocis. For myself, I believe that in the first place Tereus was a local Megarian hero and came into the story through the interconnection of Attic and Megarian legend. I doubt his becoming a Thracian much before the fifth century. It is possible that the nightingale was called "the Daulian bird" even before Tereus came into the story, but the localisation of our story in Daulis I believe to be secondary to Tereus becoming a Thracian and to be due mainly to a learned theory about the pre-Greek population of Central Greece. There is, of course, no need to examine the virtues of versions which attempt to make the best of both worlds and represent Tereus as a genuine Thracian, who pursues his wife and her sister from Thrace to Daulis, where the metamorphosis takes place.

Sophocles laid down for all time the main lines of the

[1] See Frazer's note on Pausanias, *loc. cit.*

story. The alterations of the later mythographers need not much concern us. The later Latins, for instance, for completeness' sake but somewhat nonsensically, turn the devoured Itys into a pheasant[1] or a ringdove.[2] In Ovid's account Tereus proceeds from Athens to Thrace by sea, a feature common to the version from the different source which Hyginus has preserved. Whether Ovid made Philomela the nightingale is not quite certain. His "altera" and "altera" are ambiguous. But we can hardly, I think, give him the benefit of the doubt, for presumably it was the mother whose breast was marked with the blood of the slain child, and this bird is the swallow. This aetiology for the red marks on the swallow's breast does not, I think, occur in any other version of the story. We may compare it with the legend that the swallow removed the Crown of thorns when the Saviour was hanging on the Cross; the sharp spines pricked her breast, and to this day she carries the badge of her good action.[3] Another invention of Ovid's is the Dionysiac setting given to the meeting of the two sisters: Libanius is clearly copying and improving upon Ovid.[4] Not only is there no evidence that Dionysiac rites were a feature of the Sophoclean account, but there are reasons, as Pearson shows, why it is highly improbable that they were. Welcker and Ribbeck tell us that the Dionysiac rites figured in the lost play of Accius, but

[1] Lactantius, *Narr. Fab.* vi, 7; *Scrip. Rev. Myth.* ed. Bode, *Mythog.* i, p. 2.
[2] Servius ad *Eclogue*, vi, 78.
[3] Swainson, *op. cit.* p. 53.
[4] Libanius, *Narr.* 12, p. 1103.

108

we are here in the rarefied atmosphere of speculative conjecture. That Ovid invented this feature I am pretty certain, and if we ask why he did so, the answer is not merely that Dionysiac rites are appropriate in Thrace, but further the prompting of the analogy of another story. The Dionysiac element was almost certainly suggested by the tale, connected with the human sacrifice which in a mitigated ritual form survived at Orchomenus in Plutarch's day, of how the daughters of Minyas, Leucippe, Arsinoe and Alcathoe, tore in pieces and devoured Hippasus the son of Leucippe.[1]

There are two other versions of the story which remain to be considered, both Hellenistic and both compilations. The first is the version preserved by Hyginus, 45, which Ribbeck thinks was that adopted by Livius Andronicus. Here Procne, wife of Tereus, becomes the swallow, and Philomela the nightingale is ravished. Hyginus' version, however, spares us the necessity of a tongueless nightingale, for his Tereus does not remove his victim's tongue. The plot is worked out more on the lines of a novel than of a folk-tale, and is not thereby improved. After ravishing Philomela, Tereus sent her out of the way to Lynceus. But the wife of Lynceus happened to be a friend of Procne, so she immediately sent the concubine on to the injured queen. The sisters then recognised each other and plotted revenge. In the meantime Tereus had been warned by portents that his son Itys would die by a

---

[1] The story is connected with the *Agrionia* of Orchomenus. See Halliday, *The Greek Questions of Plutarch*, pp. 164 f.

kinsman's hand. He jumped to the conclusion that his brother Dryas was plotting Itys' death and killed him. Then follows the horrid banquet prepared by the sisters and the metamorphosis. Here it is interesting that Hyginus' authority has reverted to pre-Sophoclean tradition and has turned Tereus into a hawk.

The other independent version is a compilation taken by Antoninus Liberalis (No. 11) from the *Ornithogonia* of an early Hellenistic writer who endeavoured to give his work authority by attributing it to Boio, a priestess of Delphi. To judge from this and the other specimens in Antoninus' collection, the *Ornithogonia* of Boio was an uninspired work. As a rule the author tries to get as many birds as possible into each Just-so story, and his tales are patently evolved in the study. Pandareus of Ephesus had a daughter Aedon. Here he has gone back to Homer for the names of father and daughter, but his Pandareus, like Erysichthon, is greedy as a cormorant; hence in the *dénouement* he becomes a sea eagle. Aedon married Polytechnus, a carpenter; they lived happily together and had a son Itys. So happy were they, that they must needs borrow from the tale of Ceyx and Alcyone and claim to be more loving than Zeus and Hera. In consequence, Hera sent Eris to stir up strife between them as to their respective proficiencies in their work, Polytechnus as a carpenter and Aedon as a weaver; they undertook a contest in which the loser was to give the winner a slave. The nightingale is rather inappropriately a weaver, but perhaps she has borrowed this trait from her neighbour Arachne of Colophon.

Perhaps, too, the weaving suggested itself because of the part played by the embroidered robe in the canonical version. In any event Aedon wove faster than Polytechnus carpentered; Polytechnus plotted revenge, went to Pandareus and told him that Aedon had sent him to fetch her sister Chelidonis. He then violated Chelidonis, after which he clad her in rags, cut her hair, threatened her with death if she told a word to Aedon and then gave her to his wife as the slave he had promised her as the prize of the contest. Aedon, not recognising Chelidonis, ill-treated her, until one day she heard her telling the water jug, what she had sworn not to tell Aedon, the whole story of her tragedy. This is a genuine folk-tale incident, for it is not at all infrequent in Indo-European *märchen* for the heroine, who for some good reason may not tell her story to a person, to be overheard telling it to an oven, a stone, a whetstone and knife, a glass or some other utensil.[1] After the recognition the sisters cooked Itys, and leaving a message with a neighbour that Polytechnus was not to wait supper for them, fled to their father. Polytechnus ate and then discovered the nature of the meal. He pursued them to the house of

[1] See Grimm, Nos. 89, 91, and the references in Bolte and Polívka, *Anmerkungen zu den Kinder- und Hausmärchen der Brüder Grimm*, ii, pp. 275 f. Compare, too, the story of King Midas' ears. Actually, of course, inconvenient taboos are evaded in similar ways. Thus in a village of Cappadocia, where the taboo upon a wife speaking to her mother-in-law was strictly enforced for several years, the considerable inconvenience in a patriarchal society in which married sons continue to live in their parents' house was mitigated, as I was informed, by the daughter-in-law addressing necessary pieces of information to the children in her mother-in-law's hearing.

Pandareus, but was captured by his servants, smeared with honey and exposed to the torture of flies in the sun—an Oriental cruelty, I fancy. Aedon, however, remembered her past love and kept the flies off Polytechnus, whereupon her father and brother sought to slay her. Zeus then turned them all into birds: Pandareus into a sea eagle, Aedon's mother, of whom we hear for the first time, into a halcyon, Polytechnus the carpenter into a woodpecker, the brother of Aedon into a hoopoe, Aedon into a nightingale and Chelidonis into a swallow. We may notice in this artificial compilation how poorly the aetiology works out. The birds' habits derive not from the plot of the story but from the incidental characteristics arbitrarily attributed to the persons. Aedon, it is true, repents of her quarrel with Polytechnus, but until the moral is drawn there is no indication of her grief for Itys, while Chelidonis we are told became a swallow, the friend of man, through favour of Artemis, because when losing her virginity by force and not of will, she had called loudly upon Artemis.

CHAPTER VI

PERSEUS, THE GORGON SLAYER

The tale of Perseus, the Slayer of the Gorgon, does not, it is true, provide such apt illustration of the influence of literature upon the modification of legend as do some other stories, but on the other hand it has a special interest of its own. It quite obviously is a local legend which eventually achieved Pan-Hellenic currency. It contains unique features. Nowhere else except in this context will you find the three Gorgons, or their sisters the Graeae. The legend seems early to be connected with monuments of the forgotten past, the subterranean brazen chamber of Danae and the polygonal walls of Mycenae, or with natural objects, the rocks of stony Seriphus. Finally, there is no ancient Greek hero, with the possible exception of Odysseus, the record of whose adventures is so largely indebted to episodes belonging to the common stock of Indo-European folktale as the hero of the Argolis. To the student of folktale it is therefore interesting, as indicating that a number of *märchen* motifs were in circulation at a time when the possibility of direct contact between Europe and India is very improbable.

I hope that we shall be agreed to examine the story as what it purports to be, a tale of magical adventure attaching to the name of an early pre-Dorian king of Mycenae. There have, of course, been many esoteric explanations, both ancient and modern, of the supposed hidden meaning of the tale. Ingenious arguments have sought to prove that Perseus was a sun god and the Gorgon the moon. Usener has maintained that he was the personification of summer, and his conflict with Dionysus and the Bacchanals a contest of summer and winter. Carl Robert believed that Medusa was the earth goddess. The beheading of the Gorgon is equivalent to the killing of the vegetation god. Danae also is the earth goddess fructified by the golden rain, and her father Acrisius is the mountain and citadel spirit (Berg- und Burggeist) of Argos. The weather specialists have had no difficulty in explaining the story in terms of the thundercloud. The Gorgon's bellowing is clearly the thunder, the sword of Perseus is the lightning which divides the thundercloud and releases the rain. By Rapp the single jagged tooth of the Graeae has been held to signify the forked lightning. Others, again, have explained the beheading of the Medusa as evidence that the early Greeks found the practice of scalping in vogue among the aborigines of the Western Mediterranean, and someone, I believe, has passed the pillars of Hercules and has suggested that Gorgo and gorilla are really the same word. This reminds one of the *katoblepas* or Libyan Gorgon of the natural history writers, the skin of which was alternatively described as being like a calf's or a wild sheep's. It had poisonous breath and a shaggy mane hanging over its eyes. If it shakes this aside and looks at a man—as one did when some unfortunate soldiers of Marius in the Jugurthan War attacked it— it slays him "by some natural violence which proceeds from its eyes".[1] So much for weather specialists, anthropologists and natural historians.

The euhemerists of antiquity rationalised the tale. Medusa was queen of the Amazons (Diod. iii, 52, 4 f.), or she was the daughter and successor of a Libyan king and conquered by Perseus. She was called Gorgo because of the agricultural basis (γεωργία) of her state's prosperity. Palaephatus explained that the story related to a gigantic and valuable image of Athena bequeathed by King Phorcys to his three daughters. Their guardian was called ὀφθαλμός (like the Persian "King's Eye"). Perseus, a pirate chief, captured him, and so found out where the statue was and carried it off. Another rationalistic explanation, following a favourite line, suggested that Medusa was really a hetaira. The Stoic moralists, on the other hand, explained the tale as a parable. Courage (Perseus) aided by Wisdom (Athena) will conquer fright as represented in its three kinds by Stheno = asthenia, debilitas, Euryale = lata profunditas, because terror grips the whole system, and Medusa = quasi me idusa, because terror darkens the soul and blinds the faculties.[2]

Upon these and rival interpretations of a similar general character it is hardly necessary to waste our time. Personally I agree with Plato that Gorgons, like hippocentaurs and flying horses, belong to the fantastic creations of make-believe, and with Strabo that their congeners are such bogies as Empusa and Lamia.[3]

---

[1] Alexander of Myndus *ap*. Athenaeum, v, 64, 221 B.
[2] Fulgentius, *Mit.* i, 21.
[3] Plato, *Phaedrus*, 229 D; Strabo, i, 28, 19.

That Perseus belongs in a very special sense to the Argolis there can be no doubt at all. This was certainly the view of the Greeks, and for Pindar he represents the characteristic Argive hero.[1] The same view is represented in the story of Xerxes' appeal to the Argives to remember their tie of kinship with the race descended from Perses the son of Perseus.[2] An early inscription (*I.G.* iv, 493) mentions the existence at Argos of an old and venerable corporation of ἱαρομνάμονας τοὺς ἐς Περσῆ, and to the end of antiquity Perseus and Heracles enjoyed the proudest ancestral honours among the Argives.[3] If we are right in accepting the Greek view of the nature of heroes, namely, that they were originally persons who lived and were for one reason or another canonised after death, it follows that heroes were originally local worthies, and that so far as their honour or worship became of Pan-Hellenic importance it is due to such causes as (*a*) the adoption of their legend into the canon of Pan-Hellenic mythology and (*b*) the propagation of their cult outside its native centre. Sometimes we are able to trace the main lines of this latter process, and in the case of one of the major heroic cults, that of Castor and Polydeuces, we can form a pretty clear idea of the gradual process by which it spread from its original home in Laconia.[4] Perseus did not become in the same sense as the Dioscuri a major figure of Greek cult, but in so far as he was an object of worship it is quite clear

[1] Pindar, *Isthm.* v, 41; *Nem.* x, 1.
[2] Herodotus, vii, 150.
[3] *I.G.* iv, 586, 590, 606, 940.
[4] See Farnell, *Hero Cults*, pp. 191 f.

116

that his cult radiated from its original home in the Argolis.

At Argos and Mycenae he was worshipped in historical times, and both places contained a number of memorials associated with his history. At Argos was the tumulus containing Medusa's head and the grave of his daughter Gorgophone. A tumulus of the kind which in Asia Minor would have been described as an Amazon's grave, at Argos was held to be the grave of the Maenads who fought against our hero. Mycenae, which possessed a *heroon* of Perseus, had been founded by him. Its name was popularly derived from the bellowing (μυ-κηθμός) of the Gorgons or the cap at the end of the scabbard (μύκης) which dropped off Perseus' sword. In one tradition, and apparently an old one, it had been the Cyclopes brought by Perseus who constructed the lion gate and the famous walls of polygonal masonry, hard by which was the Persean fountain.[1]

Outside Argos the cult appears to have been important in Seriphus, the island home of Perseus' boyhood in the story. This found expression on its coins and in local folk-lore, which explained the dumbness of the Seriphian frogs as due to the tired hero's indignation at being kept awake by their croaking, and the local abstention from eating lobster to the fact that lobsters had been the infant Perseus' playthings. The cult in Athens is probably late in origin and due to two causes:

[1] πόλισμα Περσέως Κυκλωπίων πόνον χερῶν, Euripides, *Iph. Aul.* 1500. The Cyclopes and the building of the walls occur in Pherecydes, probably from the epic source; the Persean fountain in Pausanias, ii, 16, 6.

(1) a confusion with Perreus, a local hero and eponym of the deme Perridae, (2) Athenian pretensions in the Cyclades. The traditional pro-Argive policy of Athens may also have had its influence. Elsewhere in mainland Greece the cult is of no importance and outside Greece it clearly went with Argive emigrants. Leaving aside arbitrary and relatively late identifications of foreign curiosities as relics of the Perseus legend—the shoe of Perseus at Chemmis in Egypt, attested by Herodotus for the fifth century B.C., or the localisation of the Andromeda episode at Joppa, which is perhaps not earlier than Hellenistic—the principal place of his worship was Tarsus, traditionally an Argive settlement.[1] From Argos the cult of Perseus had also passed to Miletus and thence in the seventh century with the mercenaries of Psammetichus II to Egypt, where the builders of the Μιλήσιον τεῖχος constructed a Περσέως σκοπή (Strabo, 801). From Miletus, too, it passed to Cyzicus on the one hand, and on the other to Iconium and the central area of Asia Minor, where Perseus became a hero of great local importance.[2] So far as the evidence of cult may bear witness, Perseus is distinctively an Argive hero, and wherever his cult is found its presence is explained either by the identification of the place with some place mentioned in the legend or by the presence of Argives.

[1] On Perseus at Tarsus and the connection of Argos and Tarsus see Farnell, *op. cit.* pp. 144, 337.
[2] See Calder, "Notes on Anatolian Religion", *Journal of the Manchester Egyptian and Oriental Society*, xi, 1924.

The late Mr Sidney Hartland has written a book in three packed volumes which bears the title of *The Legend of Perseus*. It was a pioneer work and it contains much matter which to-day would be considered irrelevant, partly because so much of what the author then sought to establish by the accumulation of examples is now accepted by social anthropologists as common form. But from the point of view of the study of the legend the book is fundamentally wrong in laying the emphasis upon the wrong part of the story. The episode of Andromeda, early though it undoubtedly is, appears to be but a secondary adventure. Primarily and in the first place Perseus is the Slayer of the Gorgon. He falls into the same category as another hero of the North-Eastern corner of the Peloponnese, Bellerophon, who slew the Chimaera.

To the tale of Bellerophon Homer alludes in a way which shows clearly that it was the theme of an epic of which he could assume his hearers' knowledge, but neither this legend nor that of Perseus belongs to the same group of traditions as that from which Homer drew his material. Like the *Odyssey*, the legend of Perseus belongs to the wonder tales of the earliest expansion of Greek navigation, but whenever we leave fairy land, the links are with the Levant and not with the Western Mediterranean nor with the Northern Aegean, nor, as in the case of the Argonauts, with the Black Sea. Again, whereas the Aeolic traditions of the Argolid belong at least in part to the Mycenaean Age, there seems to be an indication in the brazen underground chamber of Danae that the story of the miraculous birth of Perseus took its present shape at a time when the local memories of Mycenaean splendour had faded and the Beehive Tombs were rediscovered as mysterious monuments of a past epoch requiring imaginative explanation. This, also, is surely the moral of the Cyclopes of Perseus, whose magical powers were necessary to construct the great polygonal walls. It is, therefore, legitimate to suppose that the material of the lost epic of Perseus belonged to a later as well as to a different stratum of legend than that to which the older material of the *Iliad* and the *Odyssey* belongs.

Here, I think, some weight can legitimately be attached to the *argumentum a silentio*. Homer more than once mentions the Gorgon's head, a single object of terror with whose terrific aspect he and his audience are fully familiar. He nowhere connects it with Perseus. He knows, and this is interesting, the genealogy which made Perseus the grandfather of Eurystheus, and twice in the story of the birth of Heracles mentions Sthenelus as Persiades (*Iliad*, xix). The only other passage in which the Argive hero is mentioned has been suspect from the days of the great Homeric scholars of Alexandria, and even the most orthodox unitarian may regard it with suspicion. In the *Apate*, it will be remembered, Zeus rather curiously tells Hera that she is more attractive than his mortal loves and proceeds to give her a catalogue of them in the style of the Hesiodic *Eoae*. Among the ladies mentioned is "Danae of the fair ankles, daughter of Acrisius, who bore Perseus, most renowned of all men" (*Iliad*, xiv, 309). This surely is an exception which proves the rule.

On the other hand it is clear that by the time of Hesiod the story of Perseus the Gorgon Slayer was well known in Central Greece. Not only have we the description in the *Theogony* (270), but upon the *Shield of Heracles* (*Scut*, 216) was depicted the flight of Perseus in full equipment of cap of darkness, sandals of swiftness and *kibisis* from the pursuit of the immortal sisters of the slain Medusa. A favourite incident this for illustration in early art: it appeared, for instance, on the chest of Cypselus. But the Hesiodic reference, which is earlier than any surviving work of art, means that by the eighth century the story of how Perseus slew the Gorgon had become an integral part of Pan-Hellenic tradition. The cause we should have suspected to be the treatment of the Argive legend in a poem which had achieved popularity, and it is fortunate that in the mangled excerpts of Pherecydes which have been preserved by the Scholiast on Apollonius Rhodius we can trace the oldest version which we possess of the story of Perseus, and this, upon other grounds, has been attributed to a source in a lost epic.[1]

Upon one point we cannot be sure. Hesiod does not allude to the Andromeda episode, but in neither context is there reason why he need do so. In the excerpts from the second book of Pherecydes the Andromeda episode is missing. On the other hand the Scholiast on Ap. Rhod. iv, 1091 (Jacoby, i, 3, *F.* 12), which speaks of the

[1] Jacoby, *F.H.G.* i, 3, *F.* 10, 11, 12.

return of Perseus with Andromeda and Cyclopes, implies that it is to the Scholiast and not to Pherecydes that we owe the omission. With Kuhnert, I should agree that the Andromeda episode was a Greek story and not, as was until recently the general view, an importation from the coast of Palestine. With him, too, I should agree that the tale of Heracles and Hesione is a secondary imitation, i.e. a borrowing from the Perseus legend. It is certain that by the sixth century the Andromeda episode was familiar, for it is depicted upon a black-figured Corinthian vase which shows Perseus hurling rocks at the sea monster. Upon the whole, I am therefore inclined to believe that Andromeda played a part, though a secondary part, in the lost Argive epic. This is the more probable inasmuch as the main lines of the adventures of Perseus seem to have been well and truly laid in its first literary presentment. It was subsequently a popular source for themes of art and drama, but though modifications of detail, emphasis or interpretation may be traced to these and other later influences, the tradition as we have it is in essentials consistent throughout. The major change perhaps is the shifting of emphasis to the Andromeda episode from the Gorgon slaying, and that is due partly to the historical theory that Perseus was the ancestor of the Persians, which was first expressed in Hellanicus and Herodotus and is founded on the similarity of sound of Perseus and Persian, and partly to the romantic bias which found its earliest and most notable expression in the *Andromeda* of Euripides.

There is not a great deal of history to be got out of the

Argive genealogies. There are many alternative versions and, as I think is clear from the second book of Pausanias, a good deal of manipulation was applied to them in antiquity owing to the long list of names in the local Argive tradition. For instance, Perseus' sons were married to daughters of Pelops, i.e. they belong to the same generation as Atreus, father of Agamemnon, but Argive tradition knows of six generations between Megapenthes, who exchanged kingdoms with Perseus, and Orestes. It is possible also that there has been manipulation to connect the house of Danaus with the house of Pelops on the one hand and the Heraclids on the other. If we ask of what events "folk memory" has preserved a recollection, the answer is, I think, along the lines of our general criticism of how "folk memory" acts. There seems to be a recollection of one or two important and striking things, but the recollection is muddled and obscure and affords no reliable chronological indication.

First of all, there is the early connection of the Argolis with the Eastern Levant. This finds expression in the story of Io, which is much earlier than the later gloss upon it equating her with Isis and her son with Apis. The sequel to Io's eastern wanderings is the ousting of the aboriginal native dynasty descending in the straight line from the river Inachus and his son Phoroneus, the local culture hero who discovered fire and taught the arts of civilisation, by Danaus coming from the East. Danaus we may note appears to bear a racial name, though who in origin the Danaoi of Homer or of the

Egyptian list of Sea Raiders were I should not like to say. This racial name is repeated in that of the mother of Perseus. The successful usurpation of Danaus was, of course, succeeded by the episode of the Danaids and their Oriental cousins, one of whom survived to be Danaus' successor. From other sources we know that at some very early date Greek-speaking colonists passed from the Peloponnese to Cyprus, where the dialect was of the Arcadian type. Some of us believe that in the third Middle Minoan period the Argolis was invaded by chieftains from Minoan Crete. I do not think that we can definitely connect the legends of Io or of the eastern princess brought home by Perseus with the first event, nor the invasion of Danaus with the second, and I doubt if we may safely suppose, with Nilsson, that the murder of their husbands by the Danaids is founded upon the slaughter of Egyptians by women belonging to the Sea Raiders. All we can say is that local tradition preserved vague memories of very early Argive contacts with the Levant and of a deposition of the native dynasty by an invader coming over sea from the East.

Another historical fact which runs through the tradition is the rivalry of the three cities of the Argolid, Argos, Tiryns and Mycenae. This must be the fact behind the stories of the division between the three sons of Agenor, the triple division between Melampus, Bias and Proetus or Anaxagoras, the civil war of Proetus and Acrisius, or the exchanges of kingdoms such as that between Perseus and Megapenthes. Clearly there is no history of the rivalry to be got out of the tradition,

and obviously the importance of Argos has been ante-
dated.

A third important event is dimly and inconsistently
remembered in the tradition, the unsuccessful opposition
offered to the introduction of the worship of Dionysus.
This finds expression in the stories of Melampus and the
daughters of Proetus, or of Melampus and Anaxagoras,
three generations later, or again in the legend of
Perseus' battle with Dionysus and the Maenads. Here
once more we have the memory in tradition of an event
which certainly happened at some time or other. If
only we had the means of estimating approximately
when Dionysiac worship really overran Greece, many
difficulties would be cleared up. But I think, in view
of the insignificance of Dionysus in the Homeric and
Hesiodic poems, we can be quite sure that the event
did not take place in the generation assigned either to
Proetus, Perseus or Anaxagoras.

The grandfather of Perseus, Acrisius, was one of a
pair of royal twins, who, like Jacob and Esau, struggled in
the womb and subsequently fought for the kingdom.
The brother, Proetus, who was defeated in his claim to
Argos, succeeded in retaining Tiryns, which he founded.
One line of tradition is clearly unfavourable to Proetus,
and in one, perhaps later version, it was he really who
seduced Danae. On the other hand, in another line of
tradition Proetus appears to be a name to which great
events naturally become attached. In one version,
perhaps modelled on the Bellerophon story, the defeated
Proetus fled to Lycia, married, like Perseus, a foreign

princess and returned with Cyclopes to build the walls of Tiryns, just as Perseus with his Cyclopes built the walls of Mycenae. Again, Proetus is associated with the most generally accepted version of the introduction of Dionysiac worship into the Argolid, but Perseus also waged war against the invading Bacchanals led by Dionysus. I am inclined to think that Proetus and Perseus were the prominent names in the local traditions of Tiryns and Mycenae respectively, to which there was consequently a tendency in each locality to attach any major event of the past.

By arbitrarily selecting our premises from the varieties of the Argive tradition and ignoring the inconvenient variations we could spin several pretty and plausible historical theories. But if our object is to ascertain truth, they have no value at all. Like other popular traditions, the Argive has preserved vague and muddled memories of big events or movements with very little sense of chronology or order. Important happenings tend to become attached to the outstanding figures, whose stories are embellished with all kinds of folk-lore material. There is no history, I fear, to be got out of the legend of Perseus, for though we may well believe that there was a real and important pre-Dorian ruler of Mycenae called Perseus, we cannot link his name with any definite historical event or movement. There is not more history to be got out of his legend than we could get, if unaided by other sources, out of the *Nibelungenlied*, in which from other sources we know that Dieterich of Berne derives from the historical Theodoric and Etzel from Attila.

In the legend of Perseus the element of fairy tale
is predominant, though we shall notice traces of its
adaptation to the purposes of historical tradition and to
suit Greek taste. The opening is a regular *märchen*
formula. A childless monarch receives some magical
means of securing offspring, but is warned of consequences which he endeavours vainly to elude by special
artificial precautions. Here a slight adaptation has taken
place to meet Greek custom and the exigencies of the
tale. Acrisius, who has but one daughter, repairs to
Delphi to enquire about the means of securing a male
child. Though the riches of holy Pytho were proverbial
in Homer's day, this common formula of Greek legend
may be thought to be post-Homeric, belonging to a time
when the oracle was already assuming a position of
undisputed authority in Greek religious and political
life which is quite unknown to the author of the *Iliad*
and the *Odyssey*.

To prevent the untoward consequences of his
daughter knowing man, Acrisius adopts precautions
which are in general analogous to those of similarly
placed royal personages in fairy tale, though the particular form which they take is peculiar and interesting;
for the bronze tower of Horace,[1] though truer to the
general type, must surely be wrong and the version
preserved by Pherecydes the original.[2] In this the king
constructs a subterranean brazen chamber in the court-
yard of the palace, a building which, as Helbig first

[1] Horace, *Odes*, iii, 16, 1.
[2] Cf. Sophocles, *Antigone*, 944 f.; Apollodorus, ii, 4, 1.

127

pointed out, must surely be a Mycenaean Beehive Tomb. The ruins of such a structure, alleged to be the remains of Danae's prison, were still shown to travellers in the time of Pausanias.[1] It follows, then, that the story as we have it took shape at a date when the remains of Mycenaean civilisation had become inexplicable relics of a legendary past.

The precautions of Acrisius were unavailing, and although I cannot think of a precise analogue to the golden rain, it is common form in similar fairy stories for the princess to conceive the hero by contact with some magical object or substance, by smelling a flower or eating a fruit and so on. The incident is a genuine fragment of folk-tale, but again we may notice the Greek tendency to rationalise in adaptation. The golden rain is not a mere magical agent, it is really the amorous Zeus himself disguised, and, in Pherecydes, the god before the consummation of his purpose retransforms himself into his proper shape.

It is sound folk-tale tradition again which in the original version delays the discovery until the hero, now four years old, reveals his existence by the noise of his playing. The crime discovered, the nurse is put to death for her complicity. Danae and her son took sanctuary at the altar of Zeus Herkeios (possibly a later gloss on the epic), and the mother protested in vain that Zeus was the father of her child. She and her infant were exposed in a floating chest. As we have already noticed, other examples of exposure in a floating chest occur in Greek

[1] Pausanias, ii, 23, 7.

128

legend, and some have been thought to be connected with cult practice. But even if it is true that some examples of this motif are hieratic, that is clearly not the case here. The hieratic character of the floating chest incident at all is an uncertain hypothesis and it occurs as a pure *märchen* episode in Indo-European folk-tale, e.g. in the *Halfman* series of stories (Grimm, No. 54 *a*).

The chest is cast upon the rocky shores of Seriphus and is retrieved by Dictys, who bears a "speaking name", the good brother of the villain Polydectes. There are those who spin theories on the supposition that this latter name is a euphemism here for the Lord of the Underworld. For myself, if it has any significance, I should suggest that it is a "speaking name" similar to that of Dictys the Fisherman. The wicked brother is "Grab-all". The tradition that these Seriphian worthies were relatives of the Argive royal house, being descended from Amymone, daughter of Danaus, may possibly reflect historical circumstance. On the one hand, Danaus' invasion of the Argolid by sea may well have passed through the Cyclades, and on the other, the chest of Danae may have floated along the route ploughed by the keels of the eastward-bound emigrants from pre-Dorian Peloponnese. Of the Cyclades, Seriphus has no doubt been chosen for the scene because of its physical features. Certain particular rocks in that stony island were identified with wicked islanders who had been turned to stone, and to them our story bears the same relation as does the tale of Niobe to the natural features of Mt Sipylus.

In passing we may notice that theories have more than once been put forward suggesting the origin of the Niobe story in Hittite or Phrygian sculptures. They must, however, be wrong, for it is plain from Pausanias, i, 21, 5, that the weeping Niobe was the mountain itself, which from a certain angle and distance suggested the figure of a gigantic female form. "This Niobe I myself saw when I ascended Mt Sipylus. Close at hand it is merely a rock and a cliff with no resemblance to a woman, mourning or otherwise: but if you stand farther off, you will think you see a weeping woman bowed with grief." Niobe, the wicked islanders of Seriphus, the ship of the Phaeacians in the *Odyssey*, all belong to a very familiar type of local legend arising from the shape of natural objects, which suggests that they are petrified men or things.

The second chapter of the adventures of Perseus opens with the hero as a young man. The wicked Polydectes is enamoured of the surely maturing charms of Danae (similar improbability is habitually ignored in fairy tale, e.g. in *The Faithless Mother* type). Perseus is therefore an obstacle to be removed. The general lines of the tale follow approved *märchen* models: (*A*) A rash promise is exacted to perform a task which seems sure to end in the hero's destruction. (*B*) A supernatural helper comes to the rescue of the hero in despair. (*C*) He is sent to Old, Older and Oldest to find the means of accomplishing his quest. (*D*) He acquires the cap of darkness, shoes of swiftness, sword of sharpness and wallet. (*E*) With the aid of these he accomplishes his quest, escapes pursuit and takes vengeance on the wicked.

Taking these in order, it is very unfortunate that, owing to the compression which Pherecydes has undergone at the hands of the Scholiast, the details of the setting of the task are obscure. Polydectes apparently summons his vassals to an ἔρανος. In Homer an ἔρανος is a feast, either a banquet to which each member brings his own contribution (*Odyssey*, iv, 622), or a feasting in turn at the house of each member of a group of people (*Odyssey*, i, 375). The latter seems to be the true meaning of the word in historical times (e.g. Aristotle, *Eth. Nic.* 4, 2). But here it appears rather to be a case of a chieftain summoning his vassals to a feast, in return for which they are expected to present him with a gift—a form of rent dinner for which parallels could easily be found in the practice of the Lower Culture. The version in Apollodorus, which represents Polydectes as collecting goods for the wooing of Hippodamia, must be a later gloss invented for the purpose of linking up the tale with the general body of Pan-Hellenic legend. Perseus seems to have asked what present was expected, and upon being told "a horse", to have scornfully suggested "the Gorgon's Head", a vaunt which Polydectes insisted upon his making good. To the same general type belongs the version of the Argonaut story in which Pelias asks Jason, "What would you do if an oracle showed that one of the citizens was likely to cause your death?" Jason answers, "Send him for the Golden Fleece", and Pelias takes him at his word.[1]

In despair, Perseus wanders disconsolate in a desert

[1] Pherecydes, *Frag.* 105; Schol. Pind. *Pyth.* v, 133 a.

part of the island, again sound fairy tale, until a supernatural helper, Hermes, appears to comfort him with
a magical solution. By all analogy, one supernatural
helper should suffice the hero of fairy tale in such a pre-
dicament, and I am inclined to think that in the original
version Hermes alone helped Perseus to perform his
promise. But there is no doubt that Athena came early
into the story. Already in Pindar (*Pyth.* x, 70) the
goddess has ousted Hermes from the foreground, though
in Pherecydes she is rather awkwardly introduced as
getting first to the home of the Graeae and there
appearing to lend her support. Why, when there was no
need for two helpers, did Athena thus come into the tale
and then assume the more prominent rôle? There may
be several contributory causes. The main one, I think, is
that Athena was Gorgopis, and her tasselled *aegis*, like
Agamemnon's shield, bore the Gorgon's head upon it.
But if this was the real Gorgon's head, she must have got
it from the slayer of the Gorgon, and what deity so
likely to stand by this hero as the goddess who pre-
eminently helped heroes and stood by Heracles throughout his labours? Such considerations probably introduced
and gave prominence to the figure of Athena beside that
of the original divine helper, Hermes, the god who
was born in neighbouring Arcadia and was originally a
deity native to the Northern and Central Peloponnese.
Athenian interest and Athenian influence upon literature were likely rather to support than to combat her
predominance in the tale.

The first task of the supernatural helper in the legend

is true to type; it is his function to inform the hero how to obtain information as to the route to pursue in order to find the magical creature which he has to slay or the magical object which he has to procure, and how to obtain the means of carrying out his task. As a rule the hero is told to make enquiries of some aged being, who sends him on to a yet older relation, who sends him on to a third yet older and wiser—the motif which Clouston has discussed in his paper upon "Old, Older, Oldest".[1] There is perhaps a trace of the same *märchen* motif in the Homeric *Hymn to Demeter*, where the sorrowing mother enquires first of Hecate—here clearly the moon goddess—and is by her referred to Helios.

In the different versions of the Perseus stories there are here two main groups. The first is the version of Pherecydes and, I think, definitely the older. It appears also as a favourite theme of early vase painting. In this the Graeae tell Perseus the way to the Nymphs, Neides as they are labelled on vases, from whom he acquires the magical instruments for carrying out his task. In the alternative versions this intermediate stage is cut out and the Graeae are the outpost guardians of their sisters the Gorgons, who dwell in the gloomy recesses of an immense cave. In our tradition this variant almost certainly derives from Aeschylus, who may or may not have invented it himself.[2] It is due to his influence that

[1] Clouston, *Popular Tales and Fictions*, ii, p. 96; see also Bolte and Polívka, *Anmerkungen zu den Kinder- und Hausmärchen der Brüder Grimm*, ii, p. 400.

[2] Aeschylus, *Prom. Vinct.* 792 f.; *Frag.* 262; Eratosthenes, i, 22 Hyginus, *Poet. Astr.* ii, 12; Ovid, *Met.* iv, 776.

it persisted. The Graeae, to whom Perseus is sent in the first instance, are sisters of the Gorgons and, like them, malevolent bogies. They belong to the evil half of fairy land and they are known only in this context. They were born old women, the progeny of Phorcys and Ceto, a brother and sister whose union also produced Nereus, the father of the Harpies, Scylla, the Sirens, Echidna, Chimaera and the Sphinx. Their relatives declare their character. They possessed but one eye and one tooth between them, and these organs, like the Lamia's eye which she kept in a box, were detachable. They are stupid enough to be easily hoodwinked by the hero. To turn these creatures into thunderclouds is really very gratuitous. They have all the distinguishing characteristics of the bogey of fairy tale. Their detachable organs are similar to those of the witches of Lapland, and their stupidity is characteristic of such beings, who can normally in fairy tale be outwitted by some very simple ruse—pushed into the oven which they are heating for the victim or left vainly attempting to count their fingers while the hero runs away.

I do not think that there is much to be made of the variation in their number. In Hesiod they are two, Enyo and Pephredo, the latter possibly connected with φρίσσειν. In Pherecydes they are three, like their Gorgon sisters, and the name of the third is given as Deino. Such creatures are indeterminate in number and are inhabitants of fairy land, the borders of the country east of the sun and west of the moon. Variations in their localisation are not of moment. An instance of Ovid's eclecticism may, however, be noted in passing. His Graeae, like Hesiod's, are two, but like those of Aeschylus they live in the entrance of a cave, though this cave is situated not in the north-east, where Aeschylus places it, but below the ice cap of Atlas.

The entry of Atlas into the story was due no doubt to Hesiod's statement that the Gorgons dwelt "beyond the glorious Ocean on the fringe of night, where are the clear-voiced Hesperides". This led to the identification of the Neides, who possessed the magical weapons, with the Hesperides, who guarded the golden apples. Those versions which omitted the nymphs had, of course, to find alternative methods of equipping the hero, and the magical objects are either extorted from the Graeae or presented by some deity—Hermes, Hephaestus or Athena. The acquisition by direct gift from a divine helper I believe, however, to be secondary, except possibly for the sword of sharpness, which even in the version which knows the nymphs appears to be the gift of Hermes. This sword in Hesiod is the heroic falchion, ἄορ; uniformly later it is the *harpe*, ξιφοδρέπανον, or *hamus*, perhaps the Oriental scimitar.

For the student of folk-tale the occurrence of the magical objects in this very early tale is of the greatest interest, for throughout the Indo-European area they figure prominently in a number of stories. They occur normally in sets of three or four and are acquired by the hero, sometimes as a gift from a magical helper and sometimes by means of trickery from their owners or custodians. The first seems on the whole

135

more characteristic of the West and the second of the East.[1]

The shoes of swiftness in the form of winged sandals are elsewhere characteristic of Hermes. The cap of darkness—the helm of Hades—is known in other Greek contexts. It is worn by Athena in battle at Troy (*Iliad*, v, 845). According to Apollodorus (i, 2, 1, 7), the Olympians won their victory over the Titans thanks to weapons received from the Cyclopes, from whom Zeus acquired the thunderbolt, Pluto the cap of darkness, and Poseidon the trident. In the battle with the giants the cap of darkness was worn by Hermes (Apollod. i, 6, 2, 38).

The most interesting part of Perseus' equipment, however, is the *kibisis* or wallet. Its name is not Greek, it is used only of the wallet of Perseus and it occurs in the oldest records of the story. Hesychius says that it was a Cypriot word, and the Greek element in Cyprus we may remember derived their dialect from the oldest stratum of the Greek-speaking population of the Peloponnese. Professor Calder is probably right in thinking it to be an Anatolian word,[2] though it can hardly have come into pre-Hesiodic epic from Lycaonia and Isauria, for the localisation of the Perseus story in that area belongs to a very much later period. But its presence in the

[1] Bolte and Polívka, *op. cit.* i, pp. 346–361, 464–485; ii, pp. 438–440; Clouston, *op. cit.* i, pp. 72–132; Cosquin, *Contes Populaires de Lorraine*, i, pp. 50–59, 121–132; ii, pp. 79–88, 184–186, 286; Penzer-Tawney, *The Ocean of Story*, i, pp. 25–29; Dawkins, *Modern Greek in Asia Minor*, pp. 224, 265.

[2] Calder, *op. cit.* p. 26.

story does suggest that there is real fact behind the traditional contacts of legendary Argolis with the Levant.

The nature of the *kibisis* is also a puzzle. It is only used for carrying the Gorgon's head. The foolish popular etymology from κεῖσθαι and ἐσθής in Apollodorus of course represents only a Greek theory invented to explain a strange foreign word. I cannot help wondering, however, whether we may not have here another example of the alteration of a detail belonging to *märchen* in the process of its adaptation to legend. A regular item in the group of magical articles is the *tischen-deck-dich*, which at the word of command magically produces food. In the Oriental versions this is normally not a table, as in Grimm, but a table bag—the *sufra* of the modern Levant—in which provisions are carried during the day and on which they are laid at meal-times.[1] Cap, shoes, sword and wallet complete the equipment of Hesiod's Perseus and are the weapons of the original story. The mirror shield in which he views the sleeping Medusa in safe reflection is an invention of Euripides and an example of how Athenian drama affected the form of stories. The tale of the dress rehearsal of the elaborate manœuvre of cutting off a monster's head efficiently with reflected observation at a place called Deikterion at Samos is, of course, a piece of later nonsense.[2]

We come then to the Gorgons. That here and here

[1] *Journal of the Gypsy Lore Society*, Third Series, iii, pp. 157 f.
[2] *Et. Mag.* s.v. Δεικτήριον; Tzetzes, *Lyc.* 838.

only there are three and that two of them are immortal is
due primarily to the exigencies of the tale and to the
tendency towards the formation of trinities. It is in
this context only that the Gorgons have personal names.
We may perhaps notice that on Agamemnon's shield in
Homer (*Iliad*, xi, 36), upon which was embossed "a
Gorgon glaring terribly and about her Dread and
Terror", the single Homeric Gorgon has two satellites
who might easily qualify for sisters. But Homer knows
of one Gorgon only. Hector's eyes, in *Iliad*, viii, 349,
glare terribly, like the eyes of a Gorgon. The Gorgon
head itself is the ultimate terror of the underworld
(*Odyssey*, xi, 634), fear of which brings to an end
Odysseus' converse with the mighty dead. "Pale fear
gat hold of me, lest the high goddess Persephone should
send me the head of Gorgon, that dread monster, from
out of Hades." It is, of course, a theory of later speculation that this was but a shadow of the real Gorgon's
head, which remained upon Athena's *aegis*.[1]

I think myself that Gorgon was originally the name
applied to a prophylactic mask of hideous ferocity which
was depicted upon shields or buildings or town walls,
etc. The psychological basis of these practices rests upon
two complementary ideas. First, the idea at the bottom
of a great deal of savage war panoply and ritual that the
identification of such a figure with the warrior will
invest him with its ferocity as well as frighten the enemy.
Secondly, the idea which inspires a number of evil eye
amulets that something hideous or obscene will ward off

[1] Vergil, *Aeneid*, vi, 289; Apollodorus, ii, 5, 12, 4.

the influence of evil spiritual powers. Apart from the story of Perseus, the Gorgon has no existence except as a mask; there is nothing in fact but the Gorgon's head. The use of this as a prophylactic symbol and as an object of terror to increase the *mana* of warriors is sufficient explanation of its appearance on the *aegis* of Athena, the warrior goddess of the palace and citadel, the original and primary function, as Nilsson has shown, of Athena in Mycenaean times. In the Argolis, the story of how the monster to whom this head belonged had been slain, as the Chimaera was slain by Bellerophon, became attached to Perseus. Except for the Perseus story, there would never have been more than a prophylactic mask called a Gorgon's head.

Of course the original Gorgons, all three of them, were hideous. The beautiful Medusa is a romantic invention of the Alexandrian period, as is the consequential story of the contest of Athena and Medusa for a beauty prize. The Gorgons of Hesiod are clearly the Gorgons of early art—glaring eyes, grinning mouth, lolling tongue and swine's tusks are characteristic. The snake locks are later than Hesiod, whose Gorgons have snakes with upreared heads coiled round their waist.

In the original story the petrifying gaze of the Gorgon's head, after the hero, thanks to the cap of darkness and shoes of swiftness, has escaped from the immortal sisters and guardians of Medusa, is shown to Polydectes and the islanders, who remained visible to later ages as a collection of rocks. Thus the poetic justice of such tales was satisfied and there the matter ended. The more extended use by Perseus of the Gorgon's head as a weapon is late. It was introduced into the Andromeda story to slay the marine monster, which in the earliest pictorial representation is attacked by the hurling of rocks and in others is slain by the curved sword of the hero. In late versions it was used against Phineus or Agenor, to punish Proetus or as a weapon against the Bacchanals. It was used also to explain how Atlas the giant became Atlas the mountain.

The legend, too, was employed for a variety of fanciful aetiological purposes. The earliest example is Pindar's derivation of flute music from "the shrill lament that reached Athene from Euryale's ravening jaws" (*Pyth.* xii). It was the Alexandrians who saw in Red Sea coral a result of the Gorgon's petrifying gaze, or, in opposition to an alternative explanation, supposed that the venomous snakes of Libya originated in the blood which dripped from the *kibisis* during Perseus' flight.

Structurally, the Andromeda episode is independent of the Gorgon adventure, but though we cannot say definitely that it formed part of the epic, the probabilities are that it did. If it was "artificially joined on", this happened certainly at a very early date. The names, as we have noted, are Greek. It is a Greek story, not a tale borrowed from the coast of Palestine. There are those who would agree with this but would use it to support a theory equally inadmissible. The scene of Perseus' adventures, they tell us, was originally in the Peloponnese. The Gorgon was a local monster of the Argolid, as was the Sphinx of Boeotia. Cepheus, the father of Andromeda, was really the king of Tegea of that name. This theory is a variety of the doctrine of *Sagenverschiebung*, which is popular with certain German scholars, though its foundations lie in ingenuity rather than in common sense. Roughly, it supposes that all legends of which the scene is laid outside Greece are tales of events which originally happened in Greece and were afterwards localised elsewhere. There is even a school which applies this doctrine to the legends of the Trojan War and believes, for example, that Achilles first killed Hector somewhere in Northern Greece. As regards the legend of Perseus there is singularly little evidence to support this theory of local events transferred later to fairy land and the Levant. There is no known legend of the slaying of the Gorgon, the scene of which is in the Argolid. The connection of Perseus with the sanctuary of Zeus Apesantius, which claimed that Perseus founded the cult when he flew from Mt Apesas to slay the Gorgon, proves nothing at all. Local sanctuaries are quite capable of making claims quite inconsistent with received doctrine, and in Greece they frequently did so.

That Argos possessed a grave of the Gorgon's head is no indication at all that the Gorgon was ever supposed to have been slain in the Argolid. It is then argued that because Cepheus was a king of Tegea and was connected with a Gorgon's lock, the Andromeda episode originally belonged to Arcadia. Cepheus of Tegea, it is true, was given a bronze lock of the Gorgon's hair, which served as a talisman of the city—the well-known story of

Orestes' bones suggests that Tegea was addicted to talismans. But Cepheus was given this by Heracles, who has no legendary connection with Perseus whatever. The story is recorded by Pausanias and Byzantine lexicographers, and we have no reason on external evidence to suppose it very old. On internal evidence it looks late. It seems very like a combination of the motif of the prophylactic Gorgon with that of the talisman lock like that possessed by Nisus of Megara. It is just as probable, indeed more probable, that the name Cepheus was introduced into the Tegean story because it occurred in the legend of Perseus, than that the story of the rescue of Andromeda was originally located at inland Tegea and subsequently transferred to the coast of the Eastern Levant. The specific connection of the Andromeda episode with Joppa may not be earlier than Hellenistic times: the connection of the Perseus legend with Egypt is as old as Herodotus. In general, the tradition from beginning to end is consistent in imagining Perseus to have brought his Eastern bride from the far shore of the Levant. This, I myself believe, is the only piece of genuine historical tradition in the story; a reminiscence, like the legends of Io and the Danaids, of connections between the Argolid and the south-eastern corner of the Mediterranean in very early times. And to support the view that "there is something in it" there is one piece of concrete evidence—the unique non-Greek word *kibisis* which occurs only in connection with the Perseus legend and was thought by Greeks to be Cypriot.

CHAPTER VII

THE GOAT AND THE VINE

The fable of *The Goat and the Vine* raises a number of pretty problems, some of them perhaps insoluble with the evidence at present at our disposal. The fable narrates the retort of the vine to the goat which browses upon its foliage, that it will yet live to provide wine at the latter's sacrifice. The allusion is to the popularity of the goat as a sacrificial victim to Dionysus in Greek ritual usage, a fact which was currently though wrongly explained on the lines of poetic justice. Goats were sacrificed to Dionysus, *per contrarietatem* as Servius puts it, because of the damage which browsing goats did to vines. This popular, though mistaken, explanation of sacrificial usage is older than Servius and Vergil and possibly older than Theophrastus, who is presumably the source of Porphyry.[1]

The fable occurs in Aesop and Babrius,[2] but through metrical versions it can be traced to an earlier collection than these. The popularity of an epigram of Evenus of Ascalon[3] is attested by Ovid,[4] by a jest in Suetonius,[5] and by inscriptions from Pompeii.[6] Another metrical

---

[1] Vergil, *Georgic*, ii, 376–381; Porphyry, *de abst.* ii, 10.
[2] Aesop (Hahn), Nos. 404, 404 b; Babrius (Schneidewin), No. 145.
[3] *Anth. Pal.* ix, 75.   [4] Ovid, *Fasti*, i, 357.
[5] Suetonius, *Domitian*, 16.
[6] Diehl, *Pompeianische Wandinschriften*, pp. 821 f.

version is that of Leonidas of Tarentum.[1] But the approximate date of Leonidas is known. He flourished about 270 B.C. It is therefore not improbable that his source was the lost collection of *Aesop's Fables* which was published by Demetrius of Phalerum.

Having thus established the date of the Aesopic fable, as early as the third century B.C., let us turn to a fable in *The Book of Aḥiḳar*, of which the Greek fable is clearly a secondary version. Now *The Book of Aḥiḳar* was generally supposed to be a Hellenistic compilation of relatively late date, until the recent discovery at Elephantine of a papyrus containing a version of this romance which was current among the Jewish mercenaries settled by the Pharaohs at that southern guard town in the fifth century B.C. In maintaining, against the current view, that the contents of *The Book of Aḥiḳar* were old, Dr Rendel Harris had been almost alone, and it must be confessed that though he has had the rare fortune of a prophet who has been proved to be true, his original contention rested upon intuition as much as upon demonstrable evidence. Before the discovery of the papyrus, however, Smend[2] had pointed out that at any rate in some cases of correspondence, which include *The Goat and the Vine*, Aesop must have borrowed from Aḥiḳar, not Aḥiḳar from Aesop, because the Aesopic versions were demonstrably secondary. He had not noticed, however, the early date which can be

[1] *Anth. Pal.* ix, 99.

[2] Smend, "Alter und Herkunft des Achikar-Romans und sein Verhältniss zu Aesop", *Beiheft zur Zeitschrift für die alttestamentliche Wissenschaft*, xiii, Giessen, 1908.

assigned to the Aesopic version of *The Goat and the Vine*.

The Book of Aḥiḳar is a romance of which a great many versions deriving ultimately from a common source have survived in the popular literature of several nations.[1] It consists essentially of four parts: (1) The introduction, in which the aged and childless Aḥiḳar, vizier of Sennacherib, adopts his nephew and obtains the royal assent to retire from his post of vizier in his favour. (2) A series of gnomic sayings or proverbs by which Aḥiḳar endeavours to prepare the young man for his duties. (3) Aḥiḳar's disgrace is successfully plotted by the treacherous and ungrateful nephew, but Aḥiḳar is secretly saved by the person appointed to act as his executioner. The king of Egypt demands the solution of riddles on threat of war: Aḥiḳar is discovered, undertakes successfully the answering of the riddles, and is restored to favour. (4) The nephew is handed over to Aḥiḳar, who delivers himself of a series of maxims and fables directed to the topic of the righteous nemesis which eventually attends wrongdoing, after hearing which the villain swells up and bursts asunder. Sections (1) and (3) form a story frame (see above, p. 47) for (2), maxims of practical worldly wisdom, and (4), fables to illustrate the wages of sin and folly.

Of the texts later than the papyrus, which are published by Dr Rendel Harris and his colleagues, the

[1] Conybeare, Rendel Harris and Lewis, *The Story of Aḥiḳar*, 2nd ed. Cambridge, 1913. To this edition the paginal references in the text refer.

fourth section is entirely missing from the Ethiopic and old Turkish versions, but in all the others there occurs, in the fourth section, the fable of the retort of a plant to the animal which is browsing on its leaves. "Eat away," says the plant, "but when you are dead my root will be used to tan or dye your hide."[1] Its appearance in all the versions which contain at all the section to which it belongs (Syriac; gazelle and sumach tree, p. 123— Slavonic; goat and fustic, p. 21—Armenian A; goat and madder, p. 52—Armenian B; goat and madder, p. 82— Arabic; gazelle and madder, p. 156) suggests that it belongs to a prototype from which they all derive.

That the Aesopic form is secondary to this hardly needs argument, for the Aesopic form rests upon a particular Greek ritual custom, while the Aḥiḳar fable relies on the general fact that the hides of animals which eat plants used for vegetable dyes are dyed or tanned. It is easy to see how the general may have been adapted to the particular circumstance, but hard to believe in the converse process.

We have, then, reached the position that the Aesopic fable was current in the third century B.C., but that it is secondary to and an adaptation of the form of the fable which is preserved in the modern texts of *The Book of Aḥiḳar*. That these go back to a common source can hardly be denied. The attribution of this original to Democritus was formerly regarded as apocryphal only

[1] Is the emphasis upon the root in the metrical Greek versions purely an accident? Leonidas' ῥίζα γὰρ ἔμπεδος οὖσα evidently caused trouble to Paton as a translator, who renders "my stem is entire". Evenus has κἤν με φάγῃς ἐπὶ ῥίζαν.

because *The Book of Aḥiḳar* itself, previous to the discovery of the papyrus, was thought to be a late and spurious compilation.

Now the correspondence of Sharastâni's citations from Democritus with the modern Aḥiḳar books shows that the Democritean *Aḥiḳar*, which was known to him, was in fact a prototype of the modern versions.[1] But this work was in circulation in the time of Clement of Alexandria, who states in a well-known passage, Δημό-κριτος γὰρ τοὺς Βαβυλωνίους λόγους ἠθικοὺς (?) πεποίηται· λέγεται γὰρ τὴν 'Ακικάρου στήλην ἑρ-μηνευθεῖσαν τοῖς ἰδίοις συντάξαι συγγράμμασι.[2] Further, the identification of Democritus, *Frag.* 147 (Diels, *Vorsokratiker*[3]), with Aḥiḳar (p. 128, Syriac; p. 54, Armenian A; p. 158, Arabic) can hardly be doubted, when Plutarch, *de scient. praec.* 14, 129 A, is put beside Clement, *Protrept.* 10, 92, 4. The same book, which was known to Clement, passed therefore in the hands of Plutarch as a work of Democritus.

The argument then is this. *The Book of Aḥiḳar* is now known to have been in existence before 400 B.C., the latest possible date for the Elephantine papyrus. The modern versions of *Aḥiḳar* go back evidently to a common Greek prototype. This Greek prototype passed under the name of Democritus in the eleventh century after Christ: its existence can reasonably be inferred as early as Plutarch. In spite of the great authority of

[1] *The Book of Religions and Sects* of Sharastâni (A.D. 1071–1153); see Smend, *op. cit.* pp. 67 f.
[2] Clem. Alex. *Strom.* i, 15, 9.

Diels, whose third edition of the *Fragmente der Vorso-kratiker* still proclaims that the alleged Democritean *Aḥiḳar* is a forgery of the third century B.C., there is no real reason to disbelieve tradition. We may rather suppose, with Rendel Harris and Cowley,[1] that the prototype of the modern books was really compiled by Democritus (460–351 B.C.).[2] Our legitimate credulity is further supported by the fable of *The Goat and the Vine*. The prototype of the modern versions of *Aḥiḳar* contained, of course, the original and generalised version relating to the tanning of the hides of browsing animals. We know that the secondary version, adapted to the particular usage of Dionysiac ritual, was well established by 270 B.C. The Greek prototype must therefore have been earlier than this date. Indeed, if Democritus really wrote the first Greek *Aḥiḳar*, as tradition alleges, a plausible guess at the history of our fable may be ventured. Theophrastus, who was interested in sacrificial ritual and indeed is the main source of Porphyry

[1] Rendel Harris, *op. cit.* p. xcvi; Cowley, *Aramaic Papyri of the Fifth Century B.C.* p. 206.

[2] Some unnecessary trouble has been caused by the statement that Democritus translated his *Aḥiḳar* from a *stele*, a statement made not by him but about him. Cowley's suggestion (p. 207) that *stele* means a cuneiform tablet is unhappy. The counterpart is undoubtedly the golden pillars of Euhemerus' romance. But this does not mean that the Democritean *Aḥiḳar* was necessarily a *Schwindelbuch*. The fictitious documentary source is a normal piece of the romance writer's machinery. It is indeed usual in ancient Egyptian works of this general character. And as to the particular form of monument, I think that Edward Meyer (*Der Papyrusfund von Elephantine*, p. 116) was right in deriving the form of the "*Ich*" *Roman*, romance narrated in the first person, from the boastful royal monuments of the Ancient Eastern Empires.

148

upon such matters, wrote not only περὶ Δημοκρίτου but also an Ἀκίχαρος (Diog. Laert. v, 50). Theophrastus was also the master and friend of Demetrius of Phalerum, who published the first written collection of *Aesop's Fables*. Is it not probable in view of these facts that it was Theophrastus who took the fable as recorded in the *Aḥiḳar* of Democritus and gave it the special form adapted to Greek sacrificial usage? In this adapted form it was included in the *Aesop* of Demetrius and was thus common form for a poet of 270 B.C.

This detailed history of the story is, of course, but inference from probabilities, but we may take it as certain that if the *Aḥiḳar* attributed to Democritus was a forgery of the third century, there was earlier in existence another Greek version of *Aḥiḳar* which also resembled the prototype of the modern versions. It is easier to believe that tradition is right and that Democritus did in fact translate *Aḥiḳar* from an Oriental source.

We may turn next to the Aramaic papyrus, which has established the early existence of *The Book of Aḥiḳar*, unfortunately to be involved in new perplexities. The version which it records derives, according to the best opinion, from a Mesopotamian rather than a Jewish original.[1] It is, of course, fragmentary. It does not contain *The Goat and the Vine*, and this may be due to an accident of preservation. But it is remarkable how few of the fables and parables of the modern versions can be traced in the fragments of the papyrus which have

[1] Cowley, *op. cit.* p. 205; Meyer, *op. cit.* pp. 113 f.

survived.[1] Not only are the modern versions more like each other, but they are evidently more like the Democritean *Aḥiḳar* than any of them is, or the Democritean *Aḥiḳar* can have been, to the papyrus.

To this puzzle the solution which I have to suggest may at first sight appear extravagant. I am inclined, nevertheless, to believe that we have been unfortunate in the particular version of *Aḥiḳar* which has survived, in other words that the papyrus is not only fragmentary, but if complete would represent but a poor version of the romance. My reason for so thinking is this. *The Book of Aḥiḳar* certainly stands at the end, not at the beginning of a literary tradition, and, whatever historical foundation there may or may not be for the names of its characters, much of its contents must be older than Sennacherib. I do not think that this view would be controverted by anyone who has any acquaintance with such fragments of ancient Egyptian literature as have survived. Now of the four parts into which the romance of *Aḥiḳar* falls, the papyrus wholly omits section (2), the series of admonitory proverbs, just as the two poorest modern versions wholly omit section (4). The omission in the papyrus is not due to an accident of preservation, because there is a continuity of the papyrus at the point at which the proverbs should occur (Cowley, *op. cit.* p. 209). But to those familiar with the persistence of literary conventions in this type of popular book, the omission of section (2) will be significant, because sections (1) and (2) together belong to a literary formula

[1] See Cowley, *op. cit.* p. 211; Rendel Harris, *op. cit.* p. xciii.

of great antiquity. It goes back indeed to the oldest extant piece of literature, the *Admonitions of Ptah-hotep*,[1] the story of the aged vizier who gains the royal assent to the appointment of his successor and proceeds to give proverbial instruction to the young man. In view of the antiquity of that literary formula, I find it difficult to believe that section (2) was an addition made to *Aḥiḳar* at some date subsequent to that of the Aramaic version. Its absence must therefore be due to omission in a poor version.

In the papyrus, then, sections (1) and (3) run continuously. They substantiate the antiquity in the Middle East of the narrative device of the story frame and confirm the traditional narrative of the career of Aḥiḳar. The expedition to Egypt and the riddling contest are absent, but for this the fragmentary state of the papyrus may well be responsible. This is more probable than the view of Rendel Harris (p. xciii) that the missing incidents are not primitive but represent a later addition, at any rate if we are to trust in the evidence of traditional literary types. Although I do not know of an exact earlier parallel, the generic resemblance of the story in the Sallier papyrus, about the allegation of the Hyksos king that the hippopotamuses of Thebes disturbed his

[1] Like Aḥiḳar, Ptah-hotep is an historical character, vizier to one of the Pharaohs of the fifth dynasty. The earliest extant text of his sayings belongs to the Middle Kingdom, i.e. five hundred years later. The text unfortunately appears to be exceedingly difficult and I can find no reliable translation which is sufficiently complete to form the basis of real comparison. Selected passages are translated in Breasted, *Religion and Thought in Ancient Egypt*, pp. 226–237.

royal slumbers, to the incidents in this section of *Aḥiḳar* and to the corresponding portion of the *Life of Aesop* is obvious, and has more than once been noticed.[1]

[1] Gunn and Gardiner, *Journal of Egyptian Archaeology*, v, pp. 40 f.; Maspero, *Contes populaires de l'Égypte Ancienne*, 4th ed. pp. xxvi–xxvii. References are there given to some similar generic parallels in later Egyptian literature.

INDEX

Abimelech, 46
Acamas, 68
Achilles, 55, 71, 141
Acrisius, 114, 120, 124, 125, 127, 128
Actaeon, 4
Acusilaus, 78
Admetus, 52
Admonitions of Ptah-hotep, 50, 151
Aeacus, 9
Aedon, 44, 94, 96, 97, 100, 110, 111, 112
Aegeus, 104
Aegina, 9
aegis, 132, 138
Aelian, 89
Aeschines, 68
Aeschylus, 73, 82, 98, 133, 135
Aeson, 44
Aesop, 42, 46, 47, 48, 143, 144
Agamedes, 49
Agamemnon, 123, 138
Agenor, 140
Ahiḳar, Book of, 47, 144f.
Aïtylus, 95
Aladdin, 20
Alalcomeneus, 96
Alcaeus, 50
Alcestis, 52
Alcon, 19
Alexandrian compendia of mythology, 80f.
Ali Baba, 35, 48
Althaea, 48, 71, 72
Amazons, 53, 54, 115, 117
Amphipolis, 68

Anaxandridas, 80
Andocides, 68
Andromeda, 121, 122, 140, 142
animal nicknames, 101
Antoninus Liberalis, 110
Ape and the Fox, The, 47
Aphrodite, 62, 71
Apollo, 62
Apollodorus, 80, 81, 136
"Arab," 37
Arabian Nights, 31, 34, 35, 38, 41
Archilochus, 47
Architect and Apprentice, 43
Ares, 105
Argo, 4, 75
Argonauts, 18, 63, 68, 131
Argos, 117, 124, 125, 141
Aristophanes, 46, 47, 91, 100
Arta, The Bridge of, 16, 17, 31
Artemis, 62, 71, 112
Arthur, King, 17, 63
Asclepius, 11
Athena, 83, 115, 132, 135, 136, 138, 139, 140
Athenian invention of legend, 68
Athens, 99, 117
Atlas, 135, 140
Atreus, 123
Atropos, 72
Atthidographers, 79
Attic drama, influence of, 52, 73, 79, 137
Attila, 126
Aylwin, 36

elephant, artificial, 48
embroidery, designs on peasant, 21
Empusa, 115
Enyo, 134
ἔρανος, 131
Etzel, 126
Eugammon, 49
Euhemerus, 4
Eunostos, 61
Euripides, 79, 97, 122, 137
Europa, 4, 83
Eustathius, 95, 96
Evenus of Ascalon, 143
exposure in a floating chest, 55, 56, 128, 129

fables, 6, 42, 45f.
Faithless Mother, The, 130
Fates, the three, 72
Fitschers Vogel, 27
Flight, The Magical, 26, 63
floating chest, exposure in a, 55, 56, 128, 129
folk memory, limitations of, 59, 123
foundation legends, 64, 67
Foundation Sacrifice, 16
Frazer, 14, 15
frogs, silent in Seriphus, 117

games, origin of, 15
Gautama, 45
Gello, 42
Gesta Romanorum, 35
Gilgamesh, 50
Goat and the Vine, The, 143f.
Gorgon, 113, 114, 115, 120, 132, 135, 137f.
Gorgophone, 117
Graeae, 113, 132f.
graves, Amazon, 53, 117

Gray, Eva, 25
Gypsy, 24, 25, 26, 27, 41

Halfman, 129
Harpagus, 56, 103, 104
Harpalyce, 103
Hartland, 119
Hasluck, 34, 38, 43
hawk, transformation of hoopoe into, 91, 92
Hawk and Nightingale, 46
Hecataeus, 78
Hecate, 133
Hector, 138, 141
Helios, 133
Hellanicus, 78, 122
Hemithea, 54
Hephaestus, 62, 135
Hera, 71, 110, 120
Heracles, 4, 17, 53, 116, 122, 142
Herdsman, The, 32
Hermes, 132, 135, 136
hero worship, 61
Herodotus, 4, 48, 49, 50, 56, 68, 78, 118, 122, 142
Hesiod, 46, 48, 65, 77, 78, 89, 98, 101, 104, 121, 134, 135, 137, 139
Hesione, 122
Hesperides, 135
hieratic legend, 55, 128, 129
Hippasus, 109
Hippocleides, 49
Homer, 23, 52, 60, 64, 65, 72, 73, 74, 75, 78, 106, 110, 119, 120, 123, 127, 131, 138
Homeric *Hymn to Demeter*, 133
hoopoe, 9, 91, 92
Horace, 127
horse, the wooden, 48
Hurlstone Point, 65

155

156

INDEX

For EU product safety concerns, contact us at Calle de José Abascal, 56–1°,
28003 Madrid, Spain or eugpsr@cambridge.org.

www.ingramcontent.com/pod-product-compliance
Ingram Content Group UK Ltd.
Pitfield, Milton Keynes, MK11 3LW, UK
UKHW020315140625
459647UK00018B/1876